Exposing
the Dangers Behind
Martial Arts & Yoga

Many Blessings

Vith.

Prov 16:25

ENDORSEMENTS

Vito Rallo warns us in this book that one can't divorce yoga and martial arts from their evil origins in eastern occult practices. This book is timely and desperately needed. The West is being infiltrated and subtly defiled by well-meaning people who are introducing yoga and martial arts as though they could be Christianized and useful for meditation and self-defense. Vito clearly warns that can't be. Satan has blinded the eyes of many (2 Corinthians 4:4), not only unbelievers, but also Christians everywhere, so that he can slip in unawares to defile and lead them astray. Christians, I urge you to allow Vito Rallo's book to open your eyes, and then do everything you can to spread his wake-up message wherever you can. We must pull the wool off of our eyes and our friends', and learn to steer clear of the traps of yoga and martial arts, and the idolatry and defilement into which they lead. May God hear the cries of repentance and set the people free so that they may serve the one true God.

John Loren Sandford
Founder, Elijah House Ministries, Inc.
Post Falls, Idaho

In the Old Testament we read that people are perishing for lack of knowledge (Hosea 4:6) and in the New Testament (2 Cor. 2:11) we read that Paul was not ignorant of Satan's devices. It is a fact that most believers have little knowledge of the spiritual powers operating behind martial arts and yoga and, as a result, they are ignorant of how Satan is using these principles today to infiltrate western society with the deceptive spiritual principles of eastern religions. This remarkable book exposes the deceptions, which lie behind the façade. It should be required reading for every pastor and especially for all those whom God has called into the ministry of healing and discipleship. I cannot recommend this book highly enough. It will open your eyes and provide vital keys to helping those who have been trapped by the powers of darkness into spiritual bondage.

Peter Horrobin
Founder and International Director of Ellel Ministries

Dr. Vito Rallo has done the body of Christ an enormous favor by writing this book. A little hemlock, a little arsenic is all it takes to introduce destruction. The influence of martial arts and yoga upon the church has become noticeable and dangerous—opening doors to the realms of darkness that will quickly sap the life out of God's people. I have known Vito for many years now and found him to be a true gentleman and a man of great integrity. He has a fidelity to the word of God and a passion to bring life and wholeness to people everywhere. His book is timely and is backed up by someone who knows what he is talking about. Far more than a lofty dissertation, it is a practical book that we can wrap our minds around—bringing God's truth into the everyday world in which we live. This book would make a great gift to give your pastor and youth worker. Leaders need to know the real truth about these matters, and this book delivers.

Chris Hayward
President, Cleansing Stream Ministries

There is much confusion in the body of Christ concerning the topic of martial arts. I often ran into a nasty spirit of violence as I was doing deliverance on those who had been involved. After reading this very in-depth explanation of martial arts and yoga, the reason became very clear. This book is extremely well written, easy to understand, and indeed is the most thorough treatment of the topic that I have come across to date. Vito has thirty plus years in the martial arts as a student, instructor, and five-time national champion, so he knows what he is talking about. He very clearly explains the reasons why he gave up the practice, even after using it as an "evangelistic tool." I always felt this to be the way to go, but now this book gives an excellent background and experience in the topic. I highly recommend this book to deliverance workers and youth workers, as well as anyone interested or currently participating in martial arts. It is not merely an innocent sport, a physical fitness tool, or a self-defense mechanism, but it is much more!

Dr. Doris Wagner
Executive Director – Global Harvest Ministries
Colorado Springs, Colorado

Exposing
the Dangers Behind
Martial Arts & Yoga

Dr Vito Rallo

Sovereign World

Published by Sovereign World Ltd
PO Box 784
Ellel
Lancaster
LA1 9DA
United Kingdom

www.sovereignworld.com

Exposing the Dangers Behind Martial Arts & Yoga

ISBN: 978–1–85240–581–6

The publishers aim to produce books which will help to extend and build up the
Kingdom of God. We do not necessarily agree with every view expressed by the
authors, or with every interpretation of Scripture expressed. We expect readers to
make their own judgment in the light of their understanding of God's Word and
in an attitude of Christian love and fellowship.

Cover design by Simon Watkins
Typeset by Hurix Systems (P) Ltd.
Printed in the United States of America

DEDICATION

This book is dedicated to all who are searching for truth concerning the martial arts and yoga. May the truths revealed in this book both enlighten your mind and change your heart.

Acknowledgments

I want to thank my wife, Pat, first of all for her encouragement and hours of tireless editing. Also a special thank you to Doris Wagner, Eddie Smith, John Sandford, and Eric Wilson for their valuable input. I also want to thank all who read the manuscript, critiqued it, and encouraged me along the way to continue in this controversial project.

TABLE OF CONTENTS

FOREWORD

WE ARE NOW WITNESSING THE greatest explosion of supernatural and occult phenomenon ever in this earth's history! Growing interest in the pagan "spiritual" practices of all cultures is increasingly being blended with the so-called sciences.

This blend or synergy is creating an open doorway to the New Age, and eastern spirituality. And through this door, the mystical is being introduced to western society through doctors, dentists, lawyers, businessmen, and leaders in education.

Man is seeking to become supra human, and godlike in his abilities. It seems that nothing is beyond his grasp. Mankind is joining himself to the powers of the ancient world, through the eastern spiritual traditions of Hinduism, Buddhism, Taoism, and Zen.

How few realize the dark and hidden source of these powers, and who these spirits really are! These are the days foretold by the prophets of the Holy Scriptures.

"For they are the spirits of devils, working miracles, which go forth unto the kings of the earth and of the whole world, to gather them to the battle of that great day of God Almighty." (Revelation 16:14 KJV)

Now more than ever before, we need greater light to shine in the darkness. This book is such a light!

I spent 25 years as a student and instructor in the Chinese martial arts. I was recognized as a master instructor and held seven black belts in various styles of the martial arts. After that, the Lord Jesus Christ began to open my eyes. I asked Him for the Truth and for someone to help guide me to freedom—someone who also had escaped the path which I was on.

Vito Rallo of Free Indeed Ministries of Tampa Bay was just such a man. He was instrumental in the Lord's hand in breaking the chains of darkness, which had held me captive for so many years not only in my deliverance from the martial arts, but also in the restoration of my marriage and family.

This book is the long awaited guide to understanding both the dangers and occult roots of martial arts, as well as revealing the only True Source and Power to be set free!

"If the Son [of God] therefore shall make you free, ye shall be free indeed." (John 8:36 KJV)

Eric W. Wilson
www.Isaiah-Ministries.org
Johnson City, Tennessee

INTRODUCTION

THERE ARE MANY INFLUENCES IN our western society. Some are good – some are not so good. Some appear on the surface to be beneficial, but in fact, are the proverbial "wolf in sheep's clothing." In other words, the acclaimed benefits of a thing or practice of something may, in fact, turn out to be harmful, if not downright dangerous. *The irony is, it may not be obvious at the onset.*

What matters most is what lies behind the secret mask of all martial arts and yoga—what is at the root! The two are undoubtedly intertwined and are often advertised together. The practice of these activities, driven by a huge popularity factor, has made major inroads, especially of late into western society. This infiltration has had an enormous impact on our world and has become a force to reckon with because of its widespread acceptance as an innocent sport or activity.

In this book, I draw from my own experience and professional expertise of 30 plus years in the martial arts—as a former student, instructor, and later as a national champion. I will reveal what I have learned. In order to expose the myths, I will also draw on the expertise of others. I will uncover the mysteries and hidden secrets that are almost never revealed to those who are involved, or those who are thinking about becoming involved.

It never ceases to amaze me how many ignore the uneasiness they feel about getting involved in the martial arts and yoga in the first place. I think it may be because most people are not informed or knowledgeable about the spiritual roots from which these two practices originate. The deadly tentacles of deception go back thousands of years and are deeply rooted. Today, the truth is well disguised. Various forms of these two activities have now reached into all social, economic, and spiritual levels of our society. Unfortunately, warnings often fall on deaf ears and have been greatly ignored.

It is my hope that many will heed this warning, but realistically I also know, that there are those who will disagree with my assessment of the martial arts, and will probably say that there is no proof that what I am saying is true. But that itself is deception. The founders and masters of the martial arts understand what is behind these activities and will often allude to the fact that what is at the spiritual "root" is what fuels the power that one sees demonstrated. They are not themselves deceived, but they are experts at deceiving others!

I want to share what I believe is most important from my own life experiences—hard-hitting, eye-opening facts—to show where martial arts and yoga came from, how they evolved, and where they are today. Over the past six decades in particular, there has been an insidious plan being developed and implemented, which has gradually crept into the mainstream of our western society and is now affecting millions of lives to one degree or another.

What I am about to share with you in this book is not to judge or condemn any individual, or their choice to become involved in the martial arts, yoga, or any other eastern-related practice. My purpose is simply to inform all those who read this book of the truth so they may ascertain for themselves the risks of getting involved. The content of this book may shock and anger some, yet hopefully, will set others free from deception and bondage from forces most cannot fathom or understand, without true revelation.

The martial arts and yoga are often cleverly disguised as self-defense, physical fitness, a sport, exercise, stress reduction, or some other health benefit. Many are drawn to what they consider to be sheer fun, excitement, relaxation, or entertainment. Yet most who are involved in these activities and practices, even many who have been involved for years as teachers or instructors, do not have a clue what is hidden under the surface. Even if they did, most would not know what to do about it. Some would shrug it off as "no big deal" or say, "That is not possible!" Whether these eastern arts are for supposed health benefits, competition, non-competition, or self-defense, all incorporate various harmful spiritual concepts—without exception!

In recent years, these activities have exploded in popularity, running through millions of households—to schools, universities, to top government officials, and even to the White House. The eastern arts (especially yoga and transcendental meditation) have also been brought in through some medical professionals, who tout all the supposed proactive benefits that can supposedly be derived from yoga and other eastern activities.

For those involved in the martial arts and related arts, or for those who are considering becoming involved to any degree, have you ever wondered about the source of power that is behind them, or where it originates? Have you investigated, asked questions, or considered that all of these practices overlap and are integrated with each other? Have you asked who founded or created them, or what were their original purposes? *Do you want to know the truth?* Obviously, martial arts and yoga did not develop on their own out of thin air. They both have a complex root system, the knowledge of which may come as a surprise to many. Join me in taking a closer look.

CHAPTER 1

ORIGIN & HISTORY

O N THE SURFACE, THE VARIOUS eastern arts may look entirely different, have different names, functions, or purpose, but all begin from the same source and are cleverly disguised and shrouded by a veil of mystery and secrecy. The martial arts, yoga, and related arts all have the same root system—their foundation being one and the same source of power—rooted and grounded in religions, which were developed in the eastern world.

History depicts with some accuracy the early beginnings or infancy of these various art forms. The development and empowerment of these practices did not happen by accident or on their own. But they are a direct result of a strategic, long-term plan implemented by an "unseen" spirit world, operating in and through the various eastern religions of Hinduism, Buddhism, Taoism, and Zen.

Thousands of years ago, most cultures around the world found a very real need to provide protection for themselves—for self-preservation. Out of this need, they developed various methods to ensure their survival as a family. They armed themselves with weapons such as swords, knives, bows and arrows, spears, etc. for self-defense, to be used in times of danger and conflict. It was and is a natural outgrowth for basic survival.

Eastern cultures, as well, developed the use of weapons for self-defense and self-preservation. But in the process of this development, they also began to use "unarmed" methods of self-defense, which they learned through religious meditation. This was unique to eastern cultures and was not developed or found anywhere else in the world, at least not in the beginning. *The true nature and intent of these eastern arts has been shrouded in mysticism for centuries, which has covered them with a veil of deception.* This fact alone has ultimately prevented western cultures from understanding and grasping their true nature and purpose.

It is historically documented that these various fighting arts, per se, had their origins in the cradle of India and then were passed along to China thousands of years ago. Today, one can go to any library or search the Internet and retrieve volumes of related materials, depicting the history (for the most part, bits and pieces of information) about those who were responsible for the development and advancement of the martial arts, yoga, and related practices. *These practices, which have now been exported from the East to the West, are currently packaged, portrayed, and presented as very beneficial to those who engage in them!* This in itself is potentially very dangerous – both physically and spiritually.

To our benefit, however, the history and evolution is recorded and if we are willing to search it out, we will gain understanding. (If you are already involved in any eastern arts or related activities, but have uneasiness about it, I urge you to do some research yourself.)

As we begin our search in history, we see the plight of the defenseless Buddhist monks who were traveling around the country, doing whatever Buddhist monks do. We are told they were not very active and through their sedentary lifestyle, they began to gain weight—a lot of weight! If they looked anything like the big, pot-bellied statues I have seen of Buddha, it is obvious how they would be easy targets for the bandits who often beat and robbed them, who didn't care if they were holy men or not!

They had no exercise program established up to that point, but out of necessity, they had to come up with something to deliver them from their plight as easy targets! So, out of necessity, these defenseless monks began to develop skills and powers that made them far superior to the "bad-guy" robbers. My question is: How long did it take and how many times were they beaten and robbed before these mysterious powers emerged?

How long before they were able to defend themselves, as well as be able to disable or even kill their attackers? Was the killing necessary, and why?

It is reasonable to think they had the right to defend themselves, but why develop such a complex "unarmed" system? Couldn't they have used a weapon of some sort like the robbers had? Undoubtedly, most people would have! Better yet, why didn't they just appeal to their higher power (gods) to protect them? What was the point of meditation before their unseen gods if their gods could not or would not help them? Is meditation the same as prayer and if so, who and what did they receive in answer to their appeal?

There are many unanswered questions. Why is it that no other culture in the world developed similar methods to defend themselves? Many other cultures in every part of the world have had similar problems of roving bandits who beat and robbed people. Those cultures also had to learn to defend themselves in some way. Why the difference in how the Buddhist monks responded, compared to the rest of the world?

First of all, there is a vast difference between cultures in the East and in the West. Their philosophies, in general, are not parallel, but rather are in conflict with and contradict one another. Relatively speaking, very few western practitioners of the martial arts and yoga ever make the connection between these practices and their eastern roots. Most do not care about any kind of hidden spiritual link, as long as they get the so-called "benefits" they signed up for.

The history of the martial arts, as well as yoga, goes back to the dawn of civilization. Most agree that the roots of martial arts originated in India thousands of years ago, and that it eventually spread into China where it was developed more extensively. We know that in many cultures immortality and a deeper understanding of the alignment between the spiritual and the natural world were highly sought after.

Early on, these ancient people recognized that there is indeed a spiritual realm, as well as a natural. (People today, especially in western culture, do not so readily connect the two.) From the beginning, man's quest for knowledge was (and is) insatiable. In the early days, their efforts to connect the two realms would, over a period of time, lead them into various forms of meditation, through which they were able to receive both knowledge and power from an unknown, unseen spiritual source.

Yoga (including the introduction and development of all its various forms, as well as meditation) was the forerunner that would open the door to their ability to gain knowledge (the "so-called" enlightenment) of what would later translate and evolve into "the fighting arts." This would be furthered developed by Indian Buddhist monks (supposedly the "enlightened ones") who then traveled from India to China and other parts of the Far East.

There is probably some distortion and contradiction as to who did what and when it was done. But to belabor and try to sift through various opinions of trivial information such as timelines is not as important as it is to understand the spiritual aspect. Let us take a journey back several thousand years or so and examine some often overlooked facts (which are mostly ignored or counted as trivial) concerning the spiritual connection with the martial arts and yoga development from its earliest beginnings.

My point here is not to give you a history lesson or in any way portray the peoples of India, China, Japan, or other Far East countries in a negative, derogatory way. They have all contributed greatly in many different ways to the other people and societies of the world. As a people group, for the most part, they are gracious, honorable, kind, gentle, and humble. My experience and travels over the years with these people groups and cultures has been very pleasant and informative, to say the least (except in a very few instances years ago). So what I am going to share with you has to do with their religious practices and how they and their predecessors are responsible, to a great extent, for having impacted our western society today.

Their religious practices have not changed much over the span of thousands of years. Eastern cultures may vary in different ways socially and economically from each other, but their religious practices are very much intertwined and connected in similar ways and developed along many of the same lines. Now there are other cultures of the world who have also developed their own religious (or spiritual) belief systems, yet they are quite different from eastern practices and beliefs. One thing we all have in common, however, is "spiritual awareness." The main difference between the East and the West is that in most cultures of the East, people worship many so-called "specialized" deities, rather than the one true God—Creator of heaven and earth.

The similarities in the development of the various belief systems belied the fact that they were separated by thousands of miles, as well as thousands of years, as they were in the process of developing. They all believed in a spirit world. Many had beliefs in their own god, or gods. Many had several gods—the sun god, the moon god, god of Mars or other planets—the list is long! They also worshipped other created things, objects of wood, stone, etc., which were made by man's hands. The worship was in expectation of receiving favor, protection, health, and power!

In essence, man is a spirit being, housed in a human, or fleshly body. Thousands of years ago, man recognized his own weaknesses and inability to comprehend the mysteries of life and sought instinctively a connection between his own human spirit to a higher power, which could possibly lead him through life's challenges.

People in ancient Egypt recognized both the spiritual realm and the afterlife. American Indians also recognized the spiritual realm and prayed for help to what they believed was a higher power. In nearly all cultures, people recognized their "built-in" desire to communicate with and worship a power greater than their own, whom they believed could help them. Many cultures were influenced by and operated in spiritism, mysticism, and superstition. But no form of spiritual worship comes close to being as extensive and complex as the Hindu religious practices, which were developed from the cradle of their existence all the way to the present day in India. Regarding religious practices, this culture has developed differently than any other on earth.

It was India and China that would become the host countries in which the martial arts would develop. *Their openness to receive knowledge from the spirit realm, their practice and participation in spiritism and divination, along with the superstitions they embraced, made them excellent candidates for the spirit world to operate in and through.* All along, they have been, and still are, open to spiritual infusion that guides their very existence every day. But not knowing how to accurately discern in the spirit realm, they became misdirected. Both the Hindu and Buddhist religions are based on spirit worship. From the Hindu worshipper's perspective there may be a vast difference between them and Buddhism and Zen, but there is a spiritual connection, nonetheless.

Hinduism is based on the worship of approximately 300 million gods or deities, each having its own function. If the Hindu worshippers do not know what spirit to worship, they will worship all of them, just to cover all the bases. They openly appeal to any of them to assist them in their daily lives, believing that they are benign and can help them in many ways. In this way, a strong connection with their spirit realm is forged and maintained through their daily worship and meditation practices.

The Hindu religion is unique and different than all other religions. Those who practice Hinduism have three main deities that they worship:

1. Brahman (whom they believe is "the creator")
2. Vishnu (they believe to be "the preserver")
3. Shiva (known as "the destroyer")

I find it interesting that they worship one god whom they believe can create and another who can supposedly preserve, yet a third who can totally destroy them! Images of these three gods are everywhere in India. I prefer to more accurately identify these three deities as ruling principalities and powers, as is referred to in the Bible by the apostle Paul in Ephesians 6:12. I believe they are territorial in their function and these particular principalities preside primarily over India, but are gradually gaining ground and gaining power over other areas of the world, as their influence spreads and increases. I believe these same principalities rule over a vast number of lessor gods (powers) which are worshipped by untold millions of people around the world.

It was through spiritism and divination that these culture groups in India and China received instruction and knowledge from the spirit world, through methods and practices of meditation in both Hinduism and Buddhism. In modern times, an evolved form of meditation was developed by Maharishi Mahesh Yogi in 1958, known as "transcendental meditation" (hereafter referred to as TM).

This basic spiritual connection—through certain meditation practices—was the spiritual root system and foundation of all forms of martial arts, all forms of yoga, and all the related arts. As I stated earlier, the arts did not just materialize out of thin air. At the core, they were a product and result of direct human contact with an unseen spirit world—a practice that is strictly forbidden for those of the Judeo/Christian faith.

Man in karate uniform sitting in a yoga "lotus" position

Martial arts (sometimes referred to as "yoga in action" or "yoga in motion") had its earliest beginnings in yoga-type practices, which always involve meditation. The meditation *opened up the mind* to be able to receive knowledge from a dark spiritual realm. Through a perceived need and desire for knowledge, millions of people have willingly opened themselves to spirits—known to them as gods! These entities are from a dangerous spiritual realm and they are not normally seen with the natural eye, but often can be felt, sensed, or discerned in various ways. Sometimes they are called upon as spirit guides by New Agers and others.

People have willingly allowed themselves to become vehicles through which these unseen spirits can operate. These spirits (if they are allowed access) will infiltrate, control, and empower people with certain powers, which are neither natural, of human origin, nor of God. Some of these spirits even masquerade as innocent, benevolent powers, and have seduced people into believing they are there to help them in many ways.

The very foundations of Hinduism, Buddhism, and Zen Buddhism are based on occultism. Most people who understand the powers behind occultism would not go near the occult because they know the power source is evil through and through. Others who lack understanding dabble because of either ignorance or curiosity. Occult means "hidden or secret." The questions that should be answered are: Hidden from whom? Why is it hidden? Obviously, not everyone is able to discern the difference between good and evil, especially things that are well hidden and disguised.

The eastern mind, for the most part, has been conditioned to believe and accept the spiritual powers (of darkness) behind their religious practices, and they do not know who and what they are worshipping and appeasing. I personally have seen the grotesque and horrific images they bow down to at their altars and other places of worship. Many of them bow down to, worship, and appeal to these half-man, half-animal images—hoping for favor, protection, and provision.

They communicate through prayer and meditation practices, which allows these spiritual powers into their lives, which can, in turn, affect their minds, their bodies, and their will. Most people in western cultures would not think of knowingly and willingly allowing this to happen to them. Yet, they do it unwittingly through their participation in the various practices of martial arts and yoga. The "new and improved" more palatable version of Hinduism has been redefined and repackaged and is now commonly known as the New Age belief system. Is it any wonder that yoga is often practiced by many New Agers?

Seances and other occult practices also open one up in the same way. When people who call themselves mediums open themselves up through a method called "channeling," they allow what they believe to be a benign, informational spirit to reveal knowledge or to speak to them (and sometimes through them) concerning unknown things. The spirit may know of things that have happened in the past, but cannot know future events in a person's life. However, it often postures itself to be able to look into the future and do just that—foretell events that have not yet happened. People operating in these practices may or may not realize that it is a vile and dangerous evil spirit that is using them.

A few years ago, on primetime television, my wife and I saw a psychic, a medium who allowed herself to act as a channeler for a demonic spirit to speak through. As we watched, we heard the spirit take over her voice and become a deep, guttural-sounding voice speaking through her. This woman was supposedly being used by several human resource departments of companies as a valued resource for information. She was also supposedly an advisor to doctors, lawyers, and other professionals.

Imagine listening to, believing, and receiving information from the demonic realm, believing it is a good source and acting upon it! How helpful the advice was is very questionable. By the way, this same woman was later reported to have contracted non-curable throat cancer and died six months after we saw the television program.

In China, many of these same practices of spiritism and divination were already in operation when Indian Buddhist Bodhidharma came along and infused what he had also received from the spirit realm through the practice of Hindu yoga. Late in the fifth century B.C., Bod-hidharma (called Tamo in Chinese) traveled from India to China to see the Emperor. At the time, the Emperor was having the local Buddhist monks translate Buddhist texts from Sanskrit to Chinese. Their reason for doing so was to allow the general populace the ability to practice this religion. Tamo decided to travel to the countryside where many new trees had just been planted, to a temple called Shao-Lin.

There he saw the sedentary Shao-Lin monks who lacked the physical, mental and spiritual stamina to perform even the most basic Buddhist meditation, so he introduced the Indian form of yoga meditation and physical exercises. These were designed to strengthen the body, mind, and spirit of the monks. The basic exercises were based on the move-ments of the dragon, tiger, leopard, snake, and crane.

Most forms of Kung Fu (including Tai Ch'i Chuan) as well as Japa-nese Karate and others, can be traced all the way back to the Shao-Lin temple. Tai Ch'i Chuan is considered a gentle (even innocent) form of martial arts, yet the very name of it means "the ultimate fist." When it is sped up, it looks like any other form of martial arts, with both offensive and defensive techniques. Bruce Lee's version of martial arts, "Jeet Kune Do," came from the Wing Chun style of Shao-Lin temple boxing.

From the Shao-Lin Temple, martial arts would eventually be exported to other countries in the East, such as Japan and Korea, who would in turn develop their own indigenous forms. Several different methods began to be developed, and modifications were made throughout the years. At some point much later, a concerted effort began in earnest to make it more palatable and appealing to the general public, especially Westerners. A clever, strategic plan was implemented to shorten the amount of time it would take to market it to the West.

Except in a few examples, much of what was developed in India and China does not resemble what it looks like today because of so many changes along the way. It took thousands of years of evolving for it to appeal as it does today, but the exact same "powers" in the spiritual realm that introduced martial arts to mankind early on are still very much involved. None of the martial arts will work effectively without spiritual, supernatural assistance. No one knows the exact timeline when this evil spiritual realm came into existence. We do not want to overestimate or underestimate the intelligence behind the formulation of the martial arts, yoga, and other eastern arts.

These occult-based arts are the brainchild of the evil spiritual domain and they are literally inseparable from its original intent to infiltrate, influence, and eventually destroy mankind, if possible. They are nowhere close to being all powerful or all knowing (as God Almighty is), but they have certainly made great strides in detrimentally impacting the western world. Just as the human body cannot function properly without blood, neither will martial arts or yoga function effectively without the spirit that is behind them, operating in and through the human bodies of those who choose to become involved. They become one with the spiritual attachment (a little at a time or all at once).

We can change the name, but it still has the same function and purpose. *It is impossible to clean up, purify, or sanitize an occult activity.* These activities are connected to and empowered by a spiritual force that is hell-bent on controlling and dominating the human race, and will not give up without a fight. Unfortunately, a real lack of knowledge is demonstrated when people believe they can remove the original intent and purpose of the martial arts—which originally was to defend oneself—but quickly accelerated into an offensive action that was designed to do great bodily harm (rather than be harmed). Self-defense is a misnomer. *In martial arts, one must go on the offensive in order to defend oneself.* At some point, it will invariably turn into an offensive, violent action.

It is through a lack of understanding, and because of the high level of deception involved, that people fall into a proverbial pit when they embrace these so-called innocent practices of martial arts and yoga, and even try to Christianize them. Then they wonder why things are going so badly. *Just because a person does not practice these eastern religions, per se, does not make that person exempt from the spiritual effects that are rooted in and associated with these practices.*

It may not show up for years, but the seed that has been planted will one day grow. The very practice of either martial arts or yoga opens a door to the dark spiritual realm, which always, without fail, brings unwanted consequences. Consider the following analogies:

- The DNA of an oak tree is in the acorn and can only produce an oak tree, not any other kind of tree.

- An automobile will not be able to operate without fuel, and the fuel is useless without the vehicle.

- An appliance that requires electricity to operate it will not work until it is plugged into a power source.

The prevailing thought of so many, that one can separate martial arts and yoga from their original roots, or from their power source, is simply not true. Allow me to show why not.

History of Martial Arts in the U. S.

At the time World War II ended, martial arts were very rare in the United States. In fact, only Judo was relatively known, and that was because those in the military who had served time in Okinawa, Japan, had received some training in Judo outside their military bases. Upon their return to the U. S., they brought with them this new "art form," which was then later introduced to the entire armed forces on a larger scale. Few were highly trained as they are today. So, limited knowledge was passed on or taught to others.

It was in the early 1950's that the martial arts were introduced in the U. S. as a means of self-defense. Most servicemen who were trained in Jujitsu and Judo thought for the most part that they were somewhat experts. Compared to the general population, they were, but their training was limited. There were comparatively few controls in Jujitsu and so safeguards were introduced as it evolved into a competitive sport, which became known as Judo. Judo focuses on timing, speed, balance, and falling.

Judo was developed by Professor Jiguro Kano, a graduate of the Imperial University of Tokyo, Japan, who later took it to Europe in 1889. However, it would be years later before Judo became a byword in this country, after becoming the first Asian martial art to become an Olympic sport in 1964. Even in the very beginning of the introduction of martial arts into this country few, if any, really understood or questioned the spiritual connection which was covertly behind it.

Karate would be introduced later on a broad scale. Comparatively speaking, very few servicemen were being trained in Karate by the Japanese or others. Even fewer were trained enough to be truly called experts, or qualified to be instructors to train others. Lack of experience, knowledge, and expertise rendered them insufficiently qualified to pass it on to others on a large scale, as is the case today.

It wasn't until around 1952 that the Strategic Air Command of the Air Force invited a well-known instructor by the name of Hidetaka Nishiyama to come to the states and demonstrate the Karate form. They apparently thought it was fascinating and much more effective in hand-to-hand combat than any form of martial art they had ever been seen before. The speed, power, and aggressiveness performed were beyond the imagination of those who watched. Most had never seen a display of perfection and skill such as this, in both offensive and defensive positions, against opponents of all sizes, both armed and unarmed in close combat.

The U. S. military was so impressed that Mr. Nishiyama went on tour in 1953 around the country to various military bases to exhibit these techniques, which had never been seen before by the masses in our western society. By the way, the name "martial arts" was coined by the West, not the East. The word "martial" refers to something that is military or warlike in nature. It is no coincidence that one of the first areas it came into the West was through our military bases. The root word "Mars" (which we all know as the fourth planet from the sun) also refers to the Roman god of war. "Martial arts" has come to be used in the West as a general description, which would include all types and forms of eastern fighting arts.

The introduction of martial arts into our military, culminating with Mr. Nishiyama's tour, was the beginning of exposure of martial arts on a grand scale in the United States. Karate became so talked about and desired that many well-trained experts and champions were imported from Far East countries by Americans who began to sponsor them. Dojos (training centers or gyms) began popping up in every major city in the country, especially Los Angeles, New Orleans, Chicago, Philadelphia, and New York City.

One of the main problems these new instructors faced was the language barrier. They did not understand our culture very well, nor did they have very good marketing skills at that time. Most of them were college educated, however, and had many years of expert training under their (black) belts. But because of their limited marketing ability, they usually opened corner storefront buildings with a simple sign on the front with the word "Karate" in red letters.

Most people did not know what these little storefront gyms were, only that the word "Karate," written with an Oriental flair, and the emblem of a red rising sun, was somehow connected to the Japanese. Many times, people thought it was a store that sold Oriental goods, or the like, until they peeked in and saw a few students, in what looked like white pajamas, jumping around and making weird moves that were accompanied by strong noises and yells.

It took years before martial arts caught on here in America in the general public. It was not something the average person on the street wanted to do, or even know about. In fact, most people viewed these white-robed people with suspicion, as strange and mysterious, punching and kicking at something that was not there, aggressively attacking the air at full speed, with a kick or punch or other technique, and then stopping as though they had hit an unseen wall. Actually, these were known as "controlled moves," which were designed so that a person would be able to stop (or control) his technique without losing his balance or injuring his practice partner.

This was done with the precision of a gymnast or ballet dancer. These challenging moves were choreographed with such precision that indeed they were looked upon as a real "work of art," hence the name "martial arts." Some practitioners who had natural athletic ability were able to excel, but for most the training was grueling, repetitive, and extremely intense. Consequently, the majority of people that began training would only last through the one-month payment of fifteen to twenty dollars before dropping out.

Today, martial arts and yoga both have become very popular. It has been brought in one degree at a time—a little here, a little there. Now, unfortunately, a Westerner does not have to look very far to see an advertisement for either of these activities or a storefront with a sign out front. In the next chapter, I will explore just how subtly these practices evolved to where they are today.

Chapter 2

Evolution – The Yoga Connection

BEFORE I DISCUSS THE EVOLVING of the martial arts and yoga, I want to talk about evolution in general. Evolution is a hotly debated topic today. Why is the subject so controversial, and why has there been such an extraordinary effort to educate and convince people that there is no intelligent design behind the creation of all things—both seen and unseen? Many want us to believe that everything we see is the result of a "big bang" theory that came from somewhere in the cosmos—yet out of nowhere—to produce something that started the process that formed the universe and everything it contains.

Those who support the "big bang" theory believe that this really big bang out of nowhere by itself created planet Earth (over billions of years). Evolutionists believe that plants, water, and the earth's atmosphere evolved from a soupy mixture of plasma. About 3.5 billion years ago this "soup" supposedly came alive, found someone to marry, something to eat, and slowly evolved into every living thing on the planet. They believe the most basic form of life, an amoeba, somehow set the whole "life" thing in motion. The supposition is that this tiny creature (the amoeba) then had the unbelievable ability to evolve and diversify over the course of millions of years.

The theory is that this evolution was somehow able to eventually produce untold millions of varieties of living creatures (even including mankind) both male and female, of course, that would eventually over eons of time, evolve and develop and become all that we see today. All of what we see, according to them, supposedly came about (without intelligent design) with only a "big bang"—a cosmic accident—that supposedly is still expanding from nothing, yet creating something—none of which has been or ever can be proven! It is nothing but a hypothesis. Many experts are now saying there must have been a creative hand involved in this whole intricate process.

By this time you might be asking, "What does this have to do with the martial arts and related arts?" Nothing—except I am leading up to a very important point that is extremely vital to those who become involved in these arts, regarding the dangers they pose. I believe in evolution—but not in the same way as evolutionists who have invaded our educational system and have implemented their extraordinary, wild theories to convince millions of people that there is no intelligent design, or Creator, behind our existence.

The truth is that it required vast wisdom, intelligence, and power to create the universe and all it contains. There were also supernatural angelic beings created by God (prior to His creation of humans) who were given certain limited supernatural abilities, which included intelligence, knowledge, and power. Many of these angelic beings fell from favor because of their own disobedience against their Creator—God. However, their supernatural abilities were not stripped away from them. Instead, these inherent supernatural abilities have been corrupted (because of their rebellion against God) and they themselves have become evil and perverted. Their knowledge and power have been misdirected and are being misused to influence, control, and lead mankind astray, if possible—into their own rebellion and disobedience against God!

As I said in the previous chapter, it was through various meditation practices introduced by Buddhist monks that people groups in both India and China became connected to these super beings from the invisible spirit realm. These two cultures were steeped in mysticism, spiritism, and divination.

By the very nature of their beliefs and meditation practices, a channel of communication was opened through which unseen spiritual powers were given access to the minds of the Buddhist monks to instruct them.

During their times of meditation (blanking out or emptying their minds) they began to hear voices communicating with them. What voices were they hearing? They would enter into a hypnotic-type trance and use repetitive mantras to communicate with this dangerous spirit realm. What information were they given, and what were they told to do? I believe what they received was what formulated and founded their entire belief systems.

I believe what they received was what formulated and founded their entire belief systems.

Most eastern philosophy and religious belief systems claim that there is an "essential life force" which exists in the universe and is latent in every single living creature. In Hindu yoga and in all martial arts this force is a vital part. In yoga this force is known as "prana." In Chinese martial arts it is known as "ch'i," in Japanese as "ki," and in Korean, "qi." This concept has also been variously translated as "mind, spirit, energy, or life force." It can give a person a feeling of having a "sixth sense."

Almost without exception, the martial artist is introduced to the concept of "ch'i" or "ki" in training. Basically, a new entrant into either martial arts or yoga learns how to *tap into this so-called latent power* through certain required breathing exercises (which are different than normal breathing). Each person is instructed, first of all, that in order to tap into this energy or power, one must empty (or clear) one's mind and focus only on the feeling and the sound of his or her breathing exercises— inhaling and exhaling. The students are told that in order to access this energy or power, it must be practiced and developed by means of certain other physical techniques as well, which they will eventually learn.

Martial artists are told that "ch'i" or "ki" is simply the life force and inner energy that all people already possess. (Perhaps this is why many don't question where the source of this power originates.) They are indoctrinated to believe that the ability to develop, focus on, and harness this inner energy will improve the martial artist's warrior skills, as well as his ability to handle everyday problems and stresses. They are told that using "ch'i" or "ki" makes one stronger than mere muscle mass ever will. They are also told that it exists in the abdomen, and is tapped into through breathing exercises, focus, concentration, certain kinds of moves, and by frequently using the shout or yell "kiai," which means, "a focusing of ki."

Every single technique of striking, blocking, kicking, or punching incorporates the use of this energy. Every time you hear a martial arts practitioner (adult or child) using a "kiai," they are in effect using, or tapping into, the so-called universal energy force. *Not being aware of what they are actually doing, in reality, they are incorporating and using a force that comes from demonic occult powers!*

Tales abound of paranormal feats that martial artists have been able to accomplish. There are claims such as bullets being caught between one's teeth or arrows being caught by a hand in mid air. There is a claim of a punch being pulled (stopped short of striking the body) yet the effects still having been felt by the opponent. Psychokinetic phenomena (the movement of material objects by immaterial mental power) is also sometimes displayed. These accomplishments are all known as "noi cun." The source of power for such feats is said to be "ki" or "ch'i," which is widely known in the occult arts as the "life energy" or "creative force" of the universe.

Yoga

In yoga, the energy, or force, which flows through a person's body is called *prana*. This flow of *prana* is supposedly facilitated and activated through the basic postures or positions, which are called *asanas*. The correct breathing for yoga is often called *pranayama*. The twelve positions used for warm-up in yoga are actually postures of worship of the sun god.

What is known as the "seated lotus position" is one of the most popular positions and is the one that can often be seen in magazines and television commercials. It is even found on the labels and used in the advertising of women's clothing.

It is the same position that Shiva (the destroyer) is always pictured in. This position symbolizes man's supposed "spiritual evolution," and yogis say it aids the flow of the prana and the clearing of the mind when one is meditating. The repetitive mantras that are used are claimed to bring a person into a higher state of consciousness. (It isn't a higher state of consciousness; it is actually an *altered state of consciousness*.)

The same mantras are found in New Age "self-improvement" classes. Both yoga and New Age are solely products of Hinduism. You can't have yoga without Hinduism, and you can't have Hinduism without yoga. It is quite common to see people in the streets of India doing yoga poses in front of the statues of their many gods.

What is actually happening when people practice yoga (in any of its forms or under any of its names) is they are opening themselves up to a very dangerous spiritual realm. The saying of "AUM" or "OM" in yoga is actually the summoning of the Hindu deities, Brahman, "the so-called creator," Vishnu, "the so-called preserver," and Shiva, "the destroyer." The word yoga actually means "to yoke" or "bind together." The ultimate goal of yoga is to bring the practitioner into union with Brahman. By the way, Shiva is traditionally regarded as the original founder of yoga.

In the religion of Hinduism, various practices are used to enable a person to achieve the desired state of what they believe to be *nirvana* (which means a state of nothingness). They further believe that by doing so, one can escape having to live out his "so-called" *karma* in the endless wheel of *reincarnation*. Two of the practices that are used to achieve these desired results are meditation and yoga. The goal of yoga is to blank out the mind, stop all movement of the body, and cut off all sensation of the physical world (in order to bring the practitioner into union with Brahman). If *nirvana* is a state of nothingness, why would anyone want to reach it? The yogis (gurus) claim to be "gods" who have reached *nirvana*. If that is the case, why are they still here on earth?

Yoga is touted here in the West as a way to gain flexibility, reduce stress, find serenity and peace of mind, build strength, and even lose weight. All of those things sound innocent and good, and by themselves there is nothing wrong with any of these pursuits. Because yoga is often presented (in our modern western world) under the guise of science and health, people often accept it without questioning or researching for themselves. Yoga can be found under many different names, including Kundalini Yoga, Hatha Yoga, Raja Yoga, Jnana Yoga, Bhakti Yoga, and Karma Yoga. Tai Ch'i is also known as Chinese yoga.

Yoga has become so "well-packaged" as an exercise program that most people actually believe that exercise was the original intent of yoga. That is far from the truth. Yoga textbooks themselves will tell you that the various positions and the breathing exercises are for the purpose of arousing the Kundalini, which they say is the supreme cosmic energy. The exercises are designed to move the serpent force of the Kundalini up the spine to the brain, and manifest in the psychic "third eye" in the center of the forehead. When one travels to India, or when one is around Hindus, one will often see those who have a red dot in the center of the forehead, which is symbolic of that same psychic ability.

According to William Sudduth, "a quote from a Hindu Missions organization in India reads like this: 'Our mission in the West has been crowned with great success. Hinduism is becoming the dominant world religion and the end of Christianity has come near.' They claim to have 70,000 Hindu missionaries in the U.S. They're known as yoga instructors, at 20,000 locations through this nation."[1] That equates to "35-40 million people unknowingly worshiping Hindu gods,"[2] many of them claiming to be Christians! *Yoga is Hinduism!*

Recently, I heard that President Barack Obama appointed Melody Barnes as the new Domestic Policy Advisor and Director of the Domestic Policy Council. She admits that doing yoga each morning helps her get through the long days of meetings and briefings. When I googled the words "yoga in the White House," I learned that not only Melody practices yoga, but also the (now former) Chief of Staff, Rahm Emanuel, the First Lady, her two daughters, and her mother (who has now moved into the White House).

The most appalling news of all was that they arranged for yoga to be taught on the White House lawn for twelve hours, on the day of the annual Easter Egg Roll, which was held on April 13, 2009. This event has been a tradition for 131 years. I do not believe it was a coincidence to promote yoga on the most sacred of Christian holidays! One thousand children participated in this event, all under the age of ten. The instructors taught these innocent children various yoga positions and how to say "AUM," (the summoning of Hindu deities) right on the White House lawn!

This is not the first introduction of occult practices into the White House, however. There have been others, in years past, who have practiced such things as seances and astrology. But, for the most part, these practices have been done privately and not promoted to the public in the same way as this was.

The yogis are all delighted about this public endorsement and stamp of approval given by the most powerful leader in the free world, and his family. They believe this event made a statement to the world and actually built a bridge between yoga and Christianity! They also believe that the 5000 year-old Hindu practice of yoga transcends any spiritual creed or doctrine that others might have, and they see this event as a symbol of hope and the potential for unity. *However, to compromise, or forsake truth, in order to have "unity" is never God's plan, never has been, and never will be!*

According to William Sudduth, "Yoga was first introduced to the West around 1930. It was first studied in our colleges as part of Eastern Philosophy. But during the social and spiritual upheaval of the 1960's, there was a cultural revolution in this nation, and with it came an influx of Indian teachers and gurus who expounded on yoga. One of them was Maharishi Mahesh; some of his most famous and influential converts were the Beetles."[3] His other converts run the gamut from the Rolling Stones to popular actor, Clint Eastwood, among others. Mahesh is the same yogi who developed and popularized TM in this country."

Dr. Selwyn Stevens has this to say in his book, *Insights into Martial Arts:*

Marharishi stated that TM's goal is to permanently alter the mediator's perception of the world until it harmonizes with the Hindu pantheistic world view. [Pantheism means the toleration of worship of all gods.] The United States Federal Court legally identified TM as a religion in 1976, which was upheld by the Court of Appeals in 1979. "The entire mission of TM is to counter the ever spreading demon of Christianity," according to a senior spokesperson for TM in India in 1981.

Christians and non-Christians alike were encouraged to practice this form of meditation as a relief from stress, to lower blood pressure, improve mental health, improve their sex life and much more. While these may seem laudable, TM's promoters have been dishonestly saying things like "It's not a religion," and "It's a technique which won't interfere with your own beliefs or lack of beliefs, your life style or your job.

It's so beneficial, just a few minutes a day repeating the mantra will enable you to transcend all your troubles, and you will have peace, joy, good health..." and so on. These are not only bold claims—thousands who have tried TM have found it is simply not true.[4]

Yogis believe that God is an impersonal, spiritual substance, coexisting with all of reality. Pantheism is the view that everything is God, and those who believe that also believe that man is God. In the Bible, God reveals Himself as the personal Creator of the universe, and Christianity teaches us that there is a clear distinction between God and man. We are His creation, created in His image and likeness.

The Bible presents man's primary problem as a failure to conform to God's character and standards. The solution is He calls men to freely receive all the benefits of His salvation through faith in Christ alone. Yogis see man's problem in terms of ignorance, and teach one to focus on self. They believe that man simply doesn't understand that he is God, so the solution is what they term "enlightenment," or an experience with God. In order to reach that goal there is a lot of striving and effort, and they believe it may even take many lifetimes (reincarnation).

Many claim that hatha yoga is supposed to be simply flexibility exercises without the spiritual influence, but those who have been involved, and now are out of it, say that the concept of "Christian yoga" is an oxymoron. I agree wholeheartedly! It would be like saying "Christian Buddhist" or "Christian Hindu." Even the Buddhists and Hindus know that one cannot do that! You can call it Christian yoga, but it doesn't change what it is rooted in or its original intent.

Do you still want to practice yoga? Do not be deceived! "Christian yoga" does not exist—no more than "Christian homosexuality," or "Christian atheism." No matter how one includes Christian Scripture, prayer, or Christian music in the practice of yoga, it

With every compromise comes a surprise!

simply cannot be made compatible with Christianity. To attempt to do so is to compromise the truth. Not only is it compromise, but it is very dangerous spiritually, and therefore, should be totally rejected. With every compromise comes a surprise!

If you are a Christian who has practiced, or is now practicing yoga in any of its forms, and you desire to be free of any spiritual bondage brought in by this activity, you will first need to repent for your involvement. Then you will want to break the ungodly soul tie (yoke) which was formed between you and the Hindu gods. (See end of the last chapter for a suggested prayer.)

Yin and Yang

The concept of yin and yang is a Taoist belief system and is fundamental to most eastern philosophy. Yet, amazingly here in the West, the symbol of yin and yang has been gaining in popularity. It can be found in tattoos, on clothing, on signs, in advertisements, in doctor's offices, on stationery and business cards, and even on personal checks, which can be ordered from our banks. It seems to be everywhere, especially in places where martial arts and yoga are practiced. But what does this symbol really mean? Here is what Dr. Selwyn Stevens has to say about where this symbol originated and the belief system that it came out of—Taoism:

> The Taoists of ancient China believed in the existence of an energy they called "Ch'i." They claimed it flowed through the entire universe (including human bodies and organs) along invisible energy lines called

meridians. The yin and the yang are the two opposing yet harmonizing forces, which are claimed to control this energy. They do not cancel each other out nor are they antagonistic. They are parts of the whole. Both prana and ch'i are claimed to be the "essential vital force" of all creation.

In other words, the universe is god, and since we humans are part of the universe it follows we must be part of god. This spiritual concept was powerfully promoted through the cult movie series, "Star Wars" – the "Let the force (god) be with you." Many Christians, despite enjoying the general entertainment of the movies, did not agree with the spiritual message it was conveying to a largely untaught and spiritually naïve western culture. These concepts cannot be separated from their occult roots. The overwhelming evidence is that psychic energy requires a spirit or demon to operate it.

The concepts of yin and yang are both philosophical and religious. For it teaches that all things emanate, or flow from the Tao, and there are elements of this "flow" which are contrary to each other. [Supposedly] for one to achieve the ultimate is to have all things flowing in harmony.

These believers [those who believe in Taoism] claim that if an imbalance between yin and yang should occur, then illness results. Acupuncture, Reflexology, Shiatsu, and a number of other related zone therapies were developed to treat this claimed imbalance and to help restore harmony and healing. This is *psychic healing, or in other words, they use supernatural energy empowered by evil spirits*. [These same evil spirits may have caused the sickness, disease, or imbalance in the first place!]

According to the Taoists and New Age occultists, they can manipulate your body to release the "blockage of energy" in your system and then you can [supposedly] become well. Most Alternative Therapists do body manipulation, massages and even diagnostic procedures, so that by the time you come out of the clinic you feel different. Something has happened to you. What they call "energy" has been put into you. But the energy they are describing is not a natural or scientific energy…They channel a spirit into your body. We believe that is why they want to put their hands on you. It makes you feel different, because when a spirit is channeled into a human body, it causes a number of changes, including psychological and physiological, and these can even change your blood pressure so you feel different.[5]

In Chinese martial arts, the Taoist philosophy underlies all that the martial artist is taught. Taoism is essentially the belief that two worlds exist—the physical world and the spiritual world. They believe that people in the physical world can occasionally experience the spiritual world and that this contact can be sought through the use of meditation techniques. (*But to do so is to become involved in occult practices.*)

Various Chinese shamans and magicians incorporated into their own existing belief systems the ideas of Taoism, producing what came to be known as religious Taoism. The primary objective of religious Taoists was the attainment of "physical immortality!" Meditation, along with various magical practices, physical exercises, breathing exercises, and sexual practices, was considered the means of retaining vigor and achieving "everlasting life."

The yin and yang concept portrays negative and positive, darkness and light, evil and good, and death and life as opposites—yet equal forces. How can that be? How can we have things flowing in harmony that are diametric opposites? Nothing could be further from the truth. There is only one spirit realm in the atmosphere around the earth, and at the present time, it does contain spiritual forces of both darkness and light. However, the darkness and light it contains are certainly not equal forces, nor are they "in harmony" with each other!

Darkness and light are contradictory and conflicting forces, which are continually warring against each other. But good will always overcome evil, and light always exposes the darkness and causes it to flee. To believe that we could have opposite forces that are in harmony with each other is a dichotomy. Another Taoist belief is that "there are no absolutes," which, of course, is completely contradictory to the Bible.

It took supernatural beings, which were highly intelligent, to infuse these ancient eastern cultures with knowledge. The problem was, however, that this knowledge came from a very dangerous alien spiritual realm—an invisible realm, not normally seen by the naked eye. These supernatural beings needed human beings to operate through, in order to effectively accomplish their agenda. The spiritual aspect of these foundational practices of meditation and yoga (from which the martial arts would evolve) is what makes it literally impossible to separate the physical aspect from the spiritual nature of all martial arts and yoga and other eastern-related practices. It simply cannot be done no matter what type or form one becomes involved in, or what one calls it.

From ancient India these secretive methods were passed on by Buddhist monks to China, Japan, Korea and other countries and went through many changes, developments, and diversification before these arts would be openly made available to the masses. They had to evolve way beyond the original methods and training exercises used in the ancient Hindu, Buddhist, Zen, and Taoist religions, and become more domesticated and sophisticated, in order to successfully adapt enough to be accepted by the western cultures.

It would take deception of the highest level in order to mask what was truly behind the arts. (It would also take a desensitization process in the West.) The purpose of the deception was so that practitioners would not see the spiritual roots that had connected martial arts and yoga to the religious belief systems from which they evolved. Therefore, they would not be aware of any adverse spiritual ramifications. Westerners were told that they were not practicing any form of religion, i.e. Hinduism or Buddhism—that one can separate the spiritual aspect from the physical training aspect, or methods.

Nothing could be further from the truth. The one won't work without the other. Teachers, masters, instructors, and gurus know this truth and are clearly deceiving many. (In many cases, in western culture, many people have adapted and formulated their own forms of meditation and are inadvertently bowing to the same spiritual sources, which originally gave these people this spiritual knowledge.)

Those who have come out of these practices (which involved meditation) will tell you that they did experience contact with a spiritual realm. Others who remain involved are still getting information through these same spiritual powers and have an ongoing download of information, which is sucking them in deeper and deeper into a black hole, with no light in sight. Yet, they believe they are the enlightened ones—gods! That's deception of the highest level!

With this mindset and in this environment, pride becomes a huge factor. When a person gains knowledge and power from a supernatural source, that can fuel a real air of superiority over others, as well as a feeling of self-sufficiency and invincibility. Idolatry of one's instructor is also very common, as students idolize those who taught them how to acquire this knowledge and power, becoming very prideful about those who were their teachers. There is often such a deep sense of gratitude towards one's instructor that some even feel as though this person helped them "find themselves" or "made them who they are today."

It becomes a new identity! Most true martial arts practitioners will tell you it is not just an exercise program; to them it is a "way of life." Many have said they do it because, as they say, "it makes them feel complete—mentally, physically, and spiritually." Asian society has been aware of the spiritual application since early on, even coining the phrase "body, mind, and spirit" to make it more appealing. (Having been there, I can tell you that "feeling" is a poor substitute for the healing, wholeness, and the new way of life that is available through faith in Jesus Christ.)

Karate-do ("the way of the empty hand") is a form of fighting that was secretly developed on the island of Okinawa as early as the seventeenth century A.D. Gichin Funakoshi introduced Karate to mainland Japan in 1921 and he is considered to be one of the main principals responsible for modern-day martial arts. He declared his brand of Karate to be a medium for character building, with the final goal of training to be what he called the perfection of self. Within twenty years, Karate clubs had begun to be established in Japan's universities. It was introduced by demonstration to the Ministry of Education in Japan, where it was accepted, approved, modified, and taught in the education system, primarily at college levels. As a modern-day educator, Funakoshi would be successful in evolving Karate to a whole new level, by modifying the Japanese Shotokan system into a form that could be used in sports competitions.

It was in this atmosphere that Karate (in general) exploded in popularity as it was taught, promoted, and developed not just for self-defense and exercise, but as a sport for competition. Unlike wrestling, baseball, and football, etc. in the western culture, there was one huge exception—it still contained the spiritual DNA of Zen Buddhism! It was between the late 1930's and the early 1960's that some of the world's most proficient, educated instructors in the martial arts were dispatched—sent out to various parts of the world to establish Karate and its related counterparts.

I clearly remember being one of the first generation being trained (outside of Japan) by these masterful athletes and what it was like studying under these Karate masters. They, for the most part, could not speak English but that did not seem to make any difference. I willingly submitted myself to their training methods and received not only the physical training, but the same kind of spirits they had. There were times I knew I felt something was being passed by their touching me, but I didn't understand what it was until much later. In the meantime, I realized that I had become just like them. I thought it was too late to do anything about it—until years later when I was able to get free.

It wasn't until the mid 1960's that Karate caught on and began to become popular, especially on college campuses, which were very open to this new sport (obviously not knowing its history). Today, it is making inroads into our entire education system. The real thrust of popularity caught on by the general public when Hollywood began to make movies that incorporated the various styles and systems of the martial arts. This began to spark an incredible amount of interest. Hollywood gave the martial arts a "kick-start" (no pun intended) promoting further acceptance of this now-glorified violence on the big screen.

Sports tournaments began to occur everywhere. Every style of martial arts began to promote regional, national, and world championships. Even if there were only fifty people involved, they would call it a national championship tournament. Pride, arrogance, fame—to have a title now became the goal! This brought both the best and the worst athletes out in droves, along with the kooks and "wannabe" varieties, all for the sake of fame, fortune, and titles. In spite of all these efforts—tournaments, movies and the like—*martial arts still did not achieve full acceptance or respectability yet.* There was still the gut feeling and a lot of suspicion and nagging mistrust from the general public who looked at martial arts with a wary eye—and for good reason!

It was not like other sports such as football, baseball, or soccer—to name a few American sports that did not have their roots and development in Hindu and Buddhist religions. It would take a lot more work to convince people that they could separate the spiritual connection—rooted in mysticism, divination, and occult practices—and make the eastern arts more palatable and acceptable.

This would take place through the efforts of the Korean branch of the martial arts. The indigenous Korean Tae Kyon became infused with Japanese Shotokan Karate, and the resulting merger of the two produced what is known today as Tae Kwon Do. The two martial arts systems now carried the same spiritual DNA. Tae Kwon Do now has an international membership of over 20 million in 140 countries.

In 1955, it became the national martial art of South Korea. (As baseball can be said to be the national pastime of the U.S., so Tae Kwon Do is considered the national pastime of South Korea.) Tae Kwon Do would be the first to be accepted into the Amateur Athletic Union, which led to many others following suit. That led to some martial arts being legitimized as a sport in later years.

The Olympic Connection

Various Korean forms of martial arts have existed for a long time, but in the early 20th century, Tae Kwon Do became the dominant form for Korea. In 1955, a group of Korean martial arts leaders chose Tae Kwon Do as the definitive Korean martial art in an attempt to promote its development internationally. In 1973, the Korean government recognized the

World Tae Kwon Do Federation (WTF) as the legitimate governing body of the sport, and the first world championships were held in that year as a national sport. Tae Kwon Do has been part of the Summer Olympic Games since the 2000 Games, after first being accepted as a demonstration sport in 1988 and 1992, in the Olympics.

This was a huge step in the evolution process to make it more accept-able as a "so-called" innocent sport, without the spiritual baggage that had held it back from receiving full accreditation. *Through Olympic rec-ognition, it was now coated with acceptance and covered with respectability.* Now it could become a sport without much resistance in colleges and secondary schools—and even churches and synagogues.

According to an article online, "Jhoon Rhee, who is often considered to be the 'father of American Tae Kwon Do' (and who claims to be a Christian, but believes in religious pluralism and denies the deity of Christ), says that instructors have the constitutional right to teach their respective religious beliefs in their studios."[6] Jhoon Rhee creatively came out with his little jingle advertisement, "Nobody bothers me," which became famous and spread like wildfire as a catchy little tune, promot-ing his form of martial arts.

Unfortunately, once the martial arts have been fully accepted in the West, even as it is in China, Korea, and Japan (as well as many other countries) the strategic plan will almost be complete. *If all forms of the martial arts and yoga are embraced as innocent sports, beneficial exercise, or physical fitness, and given unconditional acceptance, we will see these programs being incorporated into all facets of our cultures and lifestyles worldwide.*

Some might say, "It's just a sport – physical and mental exercise – like any other sport or exercise program. What's the big deal? What harm is there in participating and engaging in these activities?" Let me ask you this: How many sports and exercise activities around the world were developed and evolved from a religion based on divination, spiritism, and ritual forms of meditation? How many are based on a foundation that evolves from and is empowered by a "so-called" universal cosmic source of power, i.e. spirit realm, spirit guides who impart knowledge and ability and power that comes only through an occult practice? The answer is "None!" Only yoga and all forms of martial arts have at their very core of existence knowledge and power based on occult practices.

Did the people who practiced Hinduism, Buddhism, and Zen Buddhism thousands of years ago (as they still do today) have more brain power and natural ability on their own to develop very complex fighting techniques such as martial arts? Did they have the ability (in the natural) to develop spiritual practices such as yoga without help from the spirit guide(s), whom they worshiped and connected with on a daily basis? Absolutely not!

Those who were, and still are involved, draw their spiritual power from those who are guiding them every day from and through a very dangerous spiritual realm. There are millions of people around the world today (through their practice of martial arts and yoga) who are engaging in various forms of the practice of Hinduism, Buddhism, and Zen *without knowing it*.

Take Muslims, for example. Those Muslims who practice martial arts (and there are many around the world who do), probably don't realize they are now practicing a religion other than Islam. That would be absolutely forbidden if one is a true Muslim! Yet, as I was researching on the Islamweb.net, I came across something I found interesting. They make a distinction between who would be allowed to practice martial arts, and who would not.

They say if one wanted to learn to show off, or earn money, or to harm others without a legal reason, that would be forbidden. However, if one wanted to learn in order to defend himself, or because he wanted to prove the power of Muslims, then learning martial arts would not only be permitted, but actually desirable, depending upon his ultimate intention. (That certainly would tie in with their intent to dominate and be superior.)

Muslims actually claim to have played a part in the development and origination of Chinese martial arts, saying that Kung Fu is part of their history and that it has been used in their spiritual cultivation. Muslims around the world acknowledge that they are using the "ch'i" and shan (in Islam known as nafas and ruh) to perform the martial arts moves.

I do not believe that the people in most western societies are aware that they are in any way tied to these various false religions directly when they engage in the practice of martial arts and/or yoga. The truth is even though it is *indirect* involvement, there is a link in the spiritual realm which cannot be denied! What took thousands of years to evolve, can actually be accomplished in one's life, spiritually speaking, in a very short period of time when one engages in the practice of either of these eastern arts! People take the bait through the deception of believing the lie—that there is no adverse spiritual connection that can cause them any harm—and then the hook is set!

There is a spiritual connection and a spiritual transfer that takes place and becomes a big part of an individual's personality and soulish realm, no matter what he or she professes to be. No longer does a person have to actually practice a false religion to be involved in it. It can be accomplished through a short cut, and that short cut is through involvement in these eastern arts! All one has to do is open that door, and the powers of deception and divination behind these false religious practices will invade one's life, because those powers have now been given the legal right to adversely affect and influence.

The evolving of the next level of martial arts has already begun through the worldwide acceptance of cage fighting, pride fighting, Tapout, and many others that are currently viewed by millions on television. What we are now seeing is the unprecedented "so-called" entertainment by athletes performing mixed martial arts techniques, which are approved by millions of desensitized, violence-oriented audiences. What has been imparted to the West has now taken on a life of its own—a giant leap forward—from kickboxing to full-contact Karate to mixed martial arts of all kinds. It has now evolved into a *blood sport* that is taking the world by storm, with caution thrown to the wind.

As far as I am concerned, the next step is obvious—to evolve to the ultimate fighting—the Arena, Coliseum, Rome, gladiators, and a fight to the death! The excitement it spurs in some people causes it to become an insatiable desire for more, which is only quenched when it is allowed to become a fight to the death. Normal sports are just not enough anymore. Even hockey began to be turned into a sport where people from the sidelines would often yell, "Kill him... kill him!" when fights broke out in the rink.

Video games have also evolved and become full of the same violence portrayed by the martial arts, and I believe we will begin to see real violence evolve in these entertainment venues, if it continues the way it is headed. If there is not an end to this, the world will see it acted out by people of all ages—the maiming and possibly even killing of innocent people.

I believe as things evolve in respect to the martial arts, they will take on more vicious content, even using weapons that will result in serious injury or death, all for the sake of entertainment, fame, and fortune. Have we digressed and become desensitized to the point at which the end result will lead us back to the coliseums of the Roman era in which gladiators killed untold numbers of innocent people—all under the guise of entertainment? If so, God help us!

Notes

1. William Sudduth, *What's Behind the Ink?* (Colorado Springs, CO: The Publishing Arm of Righteous Acts Ministries, Inc.) 2008, p. 55

2. Ibid.

3. Ibid., p. 54

4. Selwyn Stevens, *Insights Into Martial Arts,* (Wellington, New Zealand: Jubilee Resources, 2005) p.34

5. Ibid., pp 14-15

6. From website: "Enter the Dragon? (Part One: The Historical-Philosophical Backdrop)" 6 January 2009 <http://www.pastornet.au/response/articles/4.htm>

CHAPTER 3

HOLLYWOOD
OPENS THE FLOODGATES

THE ENTERTAINMENT INDUSTRY, ESPECIALLY THE movie industry, has contributed enormously to the rapid spread and immense popularity of the martial arts we see around us today. In this chapter, I will connect the dots to show who the principal actors were, how it was accomplished, and how it is still going on.

It didn't happen all at once, but once Hollywood saw the potential dollar signs at the box office, the ball started rolling. There was no stopping it. No one knew how incredibly popular these martial arts movies would become. Little by little, the martial arts were introduced into early movies such as James Bond in the 1960's. The Japanese martial arts and the Ninja cult arts were incorporated into the movie scenes, but that was just the tip of the iceberg. By this time, I was heavily involved myself in Japanese martial arts, but I didn't have a clue about what was to be unleashed in the next few years.

The 1960's was the decade in which martial arts would emerge in earnest. The test for acceptance had been passed and the flood of all kinds and forms of martial arts would become commonplace in western cultures. The Japanese systems, which are numerous, were basic, but not flashy. But they were and still are considered the "hard style," with one purpose behind them—to efficiently maim or kill an opponent. This was seen in its basic forms in the James Bond movies.

It would take more, a whole lot more, to make and promote a martial arts film that would sell at the box office. Hence the lesser known and flashier martial arts systems would emerge and become the moviegoer's choice. Kung Fu and Tae Kwon Do would take center stage. Because they are flashier does not necessarily make them less deadly. What is behind them makes them all dangerous!

Even though martial arts were introduced in the movies, little was actually known about these strange arts outside of the countries where they were developed. Very few outsiders (non-Orientals) knew or understood the true significance or the powers behind them. It took thousands of years for these secret arts to be developed and their secrets were hidden and forbidden—for the most part not to be revealed outside the countries where they were developed.

Martial arts were not revealed to western countries until after World War II, and at that time it was primarily Judo and Jujitsu. But all that has dramatically changed, and most of the civilized world has now been exposed to all forms of martial arts, yet most people in the West are still unaware of the power source behind them. It is not just physical strength alone that makes them work!

It is not just physical strength alone that makes them work!

When I became involved and started training in Karate, I sensed that something deep and sinister was in operation, but I did not understand nor was I able to put it into words. I could see and understand the physical aspects, but at times I began to wonder where I was getting the extra-sensory abilities and extraordinary power. I'm talking about supernatural stuff, such as knowing exactly what a person was going to do before he did it, or being able to answer a question before it was asked. That was psychic ability, because of the occult aspect that is part and parcel of martial arts.

At the time, however, I thought it was just a natural outgrowth of the training. But, in fact, it was a form of divination. This ability grew stronger the more I trained. So did my physical ability. I would never have imagined what was empowering me to supernaturally do these things until years later, and by that time I was in deep trouble. It took a sovereign act of God to set me totally free, and that freedom did not come all at one time.

Back to the movies—the motion picture and entertainment industry worldwide would be and still is the catalyst and main medium through which eastern religions and philosophies are being promoted and gaining popularity. But they are cleverly masked under the guise of the martial arts and yoga. It seems to me there are very few people who truly understand the spiritual ramifications—the spiritual connection that incorporates the physical and the deep occult roots—which is the basis for the power that operates through all martial arts and yoga practices. As I said before, we simply cannot separate the two—no matter what we call it, or how hard we may try to clean them up! They are permanently and intricately interwoven. An analogy of this would be that the DNA of the fruit from a tree would never be different from the DNA of the root of a tree. The fruit of anything is produced by what is at the root.

The occult powers that undergirded martial arts and yoga thousands of years ago are still present today. That truth has not changed simply because these practices have been modernized and popularized. They still cannot be sanitized because the occult influence that is at their very core simply cannot be extracted. It took thousands of years of preparation and planning to re-package and evolve these occult practices into a form that would be acceptable enough to infuse into our western society and consequently into the lives of millions of people—including Christians! (Judeo-Christian people are explicitly warned in the Bible not to practice or be involved in any way in any occult practice.)

Therefore, it would take a master plan of unprecedented proportions to entice, lure, and ultimately deceive millions of unsuspecting people to accept these practices without ever questioning where they originated or what might be behind them. That master plan was to infiltrate and influence the ignorant and the innocent alike. It was either a brilliant strategy or an incredible stroke of luck because, unfortunately, it has worked. Since I don't believe in luck, it must have been a brilliant strategy.

The movie and entertainment industry was the main vehicle that was used to implement this master plan into the West on a large scale. The process was gradually introduced and accomplished by creating an atmosphere to desensitize people to the violence, simultaneously hiding the dark side of the martial arts. Remember, it didn't happen all at once. In America, it started over six decades ago. The present-day violence, blood, and gore would never have been accepted or allowed into our living rooms (or even at the movies) years ago. It took time for it to become commonplace as it is today—fully accepted by those who agree with it and engage in it.

Some might ask, "What's wrong with the martial arts? It's innocent, good physical fitness, and builds self-confidence!" It can be good physically to a point, but there is a downside, even physically. Some of the physical detriments include arthritis, psychological and mental problems, as well as the probability of permanent injuries. I ended up with both thumbs that have limited mobility because of the cartilage damage from repetitive breaking of boards and concrete blocks. X-rays show I still have two fractured wrists that have not yet fully healed, along with some pain, which is a constant reminder of the foolishness of my past.

Let's look at one of the most influential, popular actors who starred in full-length martial arts movies—the late Bruce Lee. He was dubbed "The Little Dragon" by many and just happened to be born on November 27, 1940. According to Chinese astrological charts, this year was known as the "Year of the Dragon." Supposedly, he was born in the "hour of the dragon" as well, between 7:00 and 9:00 a.m. Thousands around the world are followers of his fame and fighting concepts. In fact, his is the first name that comes to mind when one is asked, "Who was the most popular martial artist of all time?"

Bruce Lee learned Kung Fu from his father and others. Later, he personalized his particular brand of martial arts, using combinations of several types of martial arts, as well as street fighting. The result was a style he named "Jeet Kune Do," which he demonstrated in the movies he made, and at times was asked to demonstrate at various tournaments. Jeet Kune Do means "the way of the intercepting fist." Kung Fu is a form of Chinese martial art and its roots are deeply embedded in Buddhism. Kung Fu itself has many styles and they are called by various names today. Each martial art form has a different spirit behind it, but they all have one goal and purpose in mind.

For those of you who may never see his movies, you can walk into many Karate or Kung Fu dojos (if you have enough courage after reading this chapter) and see a picture of him. You will see a half-dressed, crazed 140-pound man with a snarling, angry, contorted look, poised to attack anyone who crosses his path. I can understand seeing this picture in a Chinese dojo, but his picture can be found in non-Chinese dojos as well. (That would be kind of like seeing a picture of the Roman Catholic Pope in a Baptist church!)

Bruce Lee's portrait is honored along with other past and present masters, and even bowed down to and worshipped. (They claim they are only showing honor, not worshipping.) There is something terribly wrong with this scenario. Bruce Lee adopted many principles from Taoism and Buddhism in his lifestyle and creed, but he himself was a self-proclaimed atheist.

I wonder if anyone has ever noticed that in the posters for which Bruce Lee posed, there is a fierce, evil-looking dragon behind him, which matches his look (see image on next page). Is this a coincidence? What does that tell us? It tells me that the dragon is not just an innocent symbol. There is a deeper meaning. That evil look has an evil connection that is tied to the martial arts and Buddhism. Bruce Lee's Chinese name was Lee Siu-Loong, which means "little dragon." Having been born in the "Year of the Dragon," is it any wonder the titles of his movies almost all had the word dragon in them? Below are the names of some of his movies:

1. Way of the Dragon (also known as Return of the Dragon)
2. Enter the Dragon
3. Game of Death

So what does the dragon represent? And from where did this obscure, mythological animal come? Nearly every culture around the world from Egypt to China have as part of their culture, or folklore, a dragon (many forms of dragons actually), yet no physical fossils of dragons have ever been found! The dragon has gained much popularity in America as well, in recent years, and can be found in games, toys, videos, cartoons, on clothing, and other places. How does one explain this?

For those of you who want to take the time to look in the Bible in the Book of Revelation and investigate for yourself, the dragon is clearly identified. Here are some places you may find mention of the dragon (also referred to as the serpent at times): Revelation 12:3, 9, 13-14, 16-17; Revelation 13:2, 4, 11; Revelation 16:13, and Revelation 20:2. This dragon represents not a mythological animal, but a super-intelligent being called Satan, a powerful archangel (whose name was Lucifer before he was cast out of heaven). He is a *renegade usurper* filled with pride—the father of lies, deception, violence, and rebellion—who apparently thought he could overthrow God, who had created him. This super being is not to be taken lightly or underestimated, as some dare to.

The Bible says that Lucifer was "full of wisdom," according to Ezekiel 28:12. In the book of Isaiah, Chapter 14, it tells us that Lucifer's fall came after he decided to exalt himself higher than God and he desired to be worshiped like God. As a very powerful and influential archangel, he was able to convince one-third of God's angels to join him in rebellion. They made war in the heavenlies against God and His angels. Lucifer lost that war and, as a result, was expelled from heaven by God Himself and became known as Satan. Now the war is here on planet Earth.

This supernatural being was not and is not able to defeat God, so as a "fallen angel," he continually wages war against God's crowning achievement in creation—mankind! *Man has been given the ability to make his own choices and when man chooses to come into agreement with the ways of Satan, in essence, he chooses to come under Satan's influence.* When that happens, he no longer believes the truth of God, but now believes the lies of Satan, at which point deception occurs.

The greater the level of deception, the greater the control and influence of Satan (and his satanic forces). This deception (of mankind) began in the Garden of Eden, by the way, and has continued through the ages. Lucifer's original God-given wisdom was turned into uncanny shrewdness and cunning ability when he fell from heaven and became Satan. Over time this "dragon," (the devil, Satan) has been able to subliminally seduce man into various practices, including meditation, which brought in false belief systems—which then became false religions—all designed to direct all worship to him!

This realm is responsible for all the false religions, false worship, and occult activity that we have in our world today. Through these strategies, the devil and his hordes have been able to influence, control, and even elicit worship from untold millions of people. His subtle cunning has been and will continue to be used to deceive many—until his final demise.

By practicing any of these activities which he has introduced and created, people have willingly opened themselves up to a host of demonic entities who have physically empowered, and yes, even given knowledge (their form of education) to their willing subjects. (This knowledge from the dark side is forbidden by God because He wants us to receive knowledge from Him, not the evil one. God knows that the knowledge we gain from the dark side is designed to destroy us, not give us life.)

> Over time this "dragon," (the devil, Satan) has been able to subliminally seduce man into various practices, including meditation, which brought in false belief systems—which then became false religions—all designed to direct all worship to him!

It took thousands of years to develop and cultivate mysticism and divination through occult practices. (Divination is a cheap counterfeit of what is divine. All that is truly divine comes only from the one true God.) This is a long-term plan—initiated, perpetuated, and driven by evil spirits—which has now reached the entire world. It is nearly impossible to drive in any city in America without seeing a martial arts or yoga sign fairly often. This long-term plan—their evil agenda—is being advanced through the various forms of martial arts and yoga, and in many other ways as well!

To get back to the Bruce Lee movies, the dragon movies take on a progression of different stages. By this time, it should come as no surprise that in the second movie I mentioned, "Enter the Dragon," the *dragon enters the person through the practice of martial arts.* That should be clue number one! Through the teaching or practice of the martial arts, one can open oneself up, giving a legal right to unseen, evil spirits to enter by learning the "Way of the Dragon." (The dragon, none other than Satan, wants us to operate in his ways.) Then there was the "Return of the Dragon" which ultimately led to "The Game of Death." Do you see the gruesome progression?

Before Bruce Lee became a star, he opened a Kung Fu dojo and trained such people as actors Steve McQueen, James Coburn, and basketball star, Kareem Abdul Jabbar. Steve McQueen would later introduce now famous Chuck Norris into the movie industry.

By the way, Bruce Lee died in 1973 during the production of his last movie, "Game of Death," but the movie was finished anyway. He was only 32 years old. (By that time, he was so popular that 25,000 people attended his funeral in Hong Kong.) Rumor has it that he died in his co-star's bed and the autopsy indicated that illegal drugs were found in his system. Hmmm...drugs, violence, rage, control, demonic power, etc. Does this sound like someone you would want to emulate, or be trained by?

Bruce was haunted by his personal demons, one of which was fear. He had dreams and premonitions that he would die young, he had terrible headaches, and he sensed evil around him all the time. In the movie, "Dragon: The Bruce Lee Story," (1993) on several occasions, Bruce had to face a huge demonic entity. On one occasion, the demon knocked Bruce around for awhile and then suddenly stood there and bowed to him. Later on, the same demon turned and attempted to go after Brandon, Bruce's son. Bruce, at that point, knew he had to confront this demon (fear and all), thinking that if he did, it would not pass on as a generational thing to his son.

But just confronting one's demons does not eliminate or evict them. They have a legal right (spiritually speaking) to remain when one is involved in any form of the martial arts. They also have a legal right to be passed on to future generations simply because of involvement by one's ancestors in these activities. Bruce's father faced the same demons, as did Bruce, and subsequently, his son, because they were all involved in the martial arts.

Interestingly, Bruce Lee's only son, Brandon, also died at a young age (28) on a movie set, while filming "The Crow," yet another martial arts movie. Could his premature death have been the result of a generational curse? Brandon was only eight years old when his father died and he was later trained by one of Bruce Lee's top students, Dan Inosanto, who likely passed on more than just the training methods of Jeet Kune Do. It is likely he also passed on the same kind of spirit that Bruce Lee had, not only to Brandon, but also to others that he trained.

As far as Bruce Lee and Jesus Christ were concerned, Bruce made it clear that he was an enemy of the Lord. Even as far back as his school days in Xavier school in Hong Kong in the 1950's, he wrote in his personal diary that he had no need of God and hated having to recite the Lord's prayer at the end of each school day. Many years later, after Bruce Lee had achieved much adoration and worldly success, he was asked whether he believed in God. His response to that question was, "I believe in me."[1] He did believe, however, that mental and *spiritual* preparation was fundamental to the success of physical training in martial arts skills. So what *spiritual preparation* was he referring to?

A few years ago, I read an article that quoted David Carradine, the star of the television series, "Kung Fu," as saying that he had received Bruce Lee's spirit. I believe he received a spirit all right, but what kind of spirit? It certainly was not Bruce's human spirit, because it is not possible to get another person's human spirit. It could have been the actual demonic spirit that influenced and controlled Bruce Lee, but it was definitely a demonic spirit (or spirits) similar to the one that Bruce and untold numbers of others have received from their involvement in various martial arts.

David Carradine has been in several television commercials, one of which has him sitting in a "lotus" yoga position, elevated off the floor. That is not a coincidence, since I have already stated that yoga meditation practices were the birthplace of the martial arts. On June 3, 2009, David died at the age of 72 in Bangkok, Thailand in a hotel, while filming yet another movie. The Thai forensic pathologist who was involved in assessing the cause of his death stated that "the incident met four of the criteria for accidental death involving autoerotic asphyxiation leading to an autoerotic fatality."[2] This assessment was not surprising since it has been confirmed by two of Carradine's ex-wives that his sexual interests included self-bondage. According to the pathologist, in the end, this is what caused his death—accidental suicide.

Involvement in martial arts can indeed open one up to perversion in many areas of one's life. Sexual perversion, suicide, drug involvement, and/or bizarre behavior are not uncommon because, oftentimes, those involved seem to be pushed to the limits in many areas of their lives. It doesn't take a genius to be able to see the connection between the unseen forces, martial arts, and the resulting strange behavior.

In my earlier naïve entrance into the dragon's den (dojo), I had enough sense to know that the things I heard coming from the mouths (I think it was from the mouth) was not of flesh and blood. The sounds were not merely or solely of human origin, and there was a sinister, bone-chilling feeling that took some time to get used to. Back then, I could not identify what I was feeling or hearing, but I had some really bad vibes. Over the years, I would experience these sights and sounds thousands of times—too many to count. I would say the manifestations and actions coming through many of the martial arts practitioners (at least most of it) was not of human origin.

In Bruce Lee's films, he shrieked and made high-pitched noises while moving around, for the express purpose of throwing his opponent psychically off center. I'm not sure if the weird noises and facial contortions were made because of the fear he himself had, or if it was because what was operating in him was trying to put fear into his opponent. I would say it was a combination of both. Many I have witnessed over the years made noises like Bruce Lee did—animal sounds. At times, it sounded crazed and weird, with extended screams, facial contortions, and weird body movements. Sometimes it was cat-like sounds, or high-pitched monkey sounds. At other times, it was deep, guttural sounds. All of these had a purpose, some of which were:

1. To intimidate

2. To throw one's opponent off focus

3. To try to put incredible fear into another person

4. To bring up and use the "so-called" hidden power source (ki or ch'i) which is always connected to many of these sounds, expressions, and movements

What you hear and see coming from a person is often not as dangerous or scary as what you don't see. The hidden, unseen force is the one to discern and be aware of.

America's Hollywood today, as well as China and other countries, are producing some of the most ridiculous, bizarre movies imaginable. Actors are performing super feats, such as flying from rooftop to rooftop, fighting and beating twenty-five or thirty attackers at a time, or dodging bullets, spears, arrows, knives, or swords. The wonders never cease to amaze me. That's entertainment, or is it? Some people, because they are so deceived from watching this kind of thing long enough, actually believe they also can do some of these crazy feats, if they practice long enough and hard enough. That is nothing but deception.

I remember a self-trained young man who used to roll off roofs, apparently believing he could not get hurt. He was one of those Bruce Lee "wannabes" who entered one of my tournaments. He screamed and jumped at one of my better students in a competition match. Before his "Bruce Lee" scream was completed, he paid the price and got flattened very quickly. I have seen this kind of behavior many times in many tournaments over the years. They want to emulate Bruce Lee and intimidate as he did. But, interestingly, Bruce Lee himself never entered formal tournament competition!

You can train and practice as hard as you want and as long as you want, but you are not going to defy the law of physics and fly, unless you are in some type of aircraft. Nor are you going to defeat twenty-five attackers at one time or even ten, or five. You will notice in the movies they don't all attack at one time. It is one at a time, or that person would be easily overcome, or dead. It is Hollywood's form of violence-related fantasy.

There are evil spirits attached to all forms of martial arts—dragon spirits, snake spirits, animal spirits, etc. Each form of martial arts has its own set of spirits. They all manifest differently. The symbol used by many Karate schools is the snake, in most cases the cobra. But, overall, the most common symbol used is the dragon. If you remember, in the movie, "The Karate Kid," the mean, nasty school wore the symbol of the cobra. The instructor and the students all had a very bad attitude. The movie was unrealistic (as many movies are) yet many found it entertaining because it portrayed the young man who played the Karate kid as the good guy, which helped give Karate a "good-guy image."

Hollywood black belts are numerous, one of which was Elvis Presley. One could clearly see his Karate-training moves when he was performing on stage. There was Van Damme, portrayed as a nice guy, but in violent movies. Then there is Chuck Norris, who professes to be a Christian, as many do who practice martial arts. Chuck's official website has this to say about him:

> When you think of Chuck Norris, you either immediately think action movie star (recalling his numerous feature films) or television star, for his long-running CBS television series, "Walker, Texas Ranger." But prior to that, Chuck was a martial arts star, winning many martial arts championships, including being a six-time undefeated World Professional Middle-Weight Karate Champion. Chuck was also a renowned teacher in the martial arts. Some of his students were Steve McQueen, Bob Barker, Priscilla Presley, and Donnie and Marie Osmond...Chuck is also founder and President of United Fighting Arts Federation, with over 2300 black belts all over the world.

In 1997, Chuck achieved another milestone in his life by being the first man ever in the Western Hemisphere to be awarded an 8th degree Black Belt Grand Master recognition in the Tae Kwon Do system. This was a first in 4,500 years of tradition…In 1988, Chuck wrote his autobiography, *The Secret of Inner Strength*, for Little Brown Publishing, which became a New York Times Best Seller. He followed up a few years later with a second book, *The Secret Power Within: Zen Solutions to Real Problems*, also with Little Brown Publishing.[3]

Chuck's site states that his 8th degree Black Belt Grand Master recognition in the Tae Kwon Do system was a "first in 4,500 years of tradition," but how can that be when Tae Kwon Do has only been around since 1955? The indigenous forms in Korea were called Tae Kyon.During the years of Korea's suppression, General Choi Hong Hi claims to have learned Tae Kyon from a famous Korean calligrapher. He later studied Shotokan Karate in Kyoto, Japan. After the 1945 liberation of Korea, General Choi introduced Tae Kwon Do—which he himself created—to the newly established South Korean army. He considers his style to be a hybrid of Tae Kyon and Karate. That's why it is sometimes called Korean Karate rather than Tae Kwon Do.

At some point, Chuck apparently found Jesus Christ. My question is: How can anyone claim to be a Christian and continue to practice Zen—a false religion? I don't know anything about his Christian conversion, but I do know one thing. Christianity and demonic activities don't mix. Chuck Norris claims on his own site that he is an 8th degree master. What's wrong with this picture? He goes behind the pulpit in many churches to proclaim Jesus is the "Master," yet it appears he is attempting to serve two masters. I am not questioning the sincerity of his profession of faith and belief in Jesus Christ, but Jesus Himself said that we cannot serve two masters—that we would either love the one and hate the other, or vice versa. I truly believe that Chuck is sincere, kind, likeable, and generous. But any of us can be sincere and be sincerely wrong!

At the very least, there seems to be a dangerous mixture, which any of us can have if we have never received deliverance (from strongholds of evil) after we become a Christian. I, too, had a similar experience. If a person's identity is wrapped up in what he believed before he became a Christian, sometimes it is hard to let go of that "identity." If it is such a big part of who a person is, he may not realize the ill effects of his previous involvement, and it may be difficult to fully embrace the whole truth of Christianity.

The result is an unholy mixture and *to those who are reading our lives it can be very confusing*, to say the least! This can be especially detrimental if we just happen to be a very well known, influential person. The Word of God says that true light has no fellowship with darkness.

In addition to the accolades mentioned above, Chuck founded an organization in 1990 called "Kick Start," originally named, "Kick Drugs Out of America." It now has approximately 4200 active participants, according to his website. His stated purpose is "helping youngsters resist drug-related peer pressures through martial arts training"[4] where is he involved in helping them gain a "strong sense of self-awareness and inner strength."[5]

What happened to God-awareness and the strength that comes from being united with Him through His Son, Jesus? Chuck's site continues by saying, "In addition, martial arts training provides them with the core values and philosophies associated with leading a productive and healthy life."[6] The last time I checked my Bible, it said that as Christians we are to get our core values from the Word of God and depart from all philosophies that don't line up with God's Word.

It amazes me that big-name ministries such as T. D. Jakes are having him in to speak, and Christian magazines are putting him on their cover. In 2008, he openly endorsed a well-known Christian politician, the very likeable and well-qualified, former governor Mike Huckabee, who just happened to be running for president of the United States.

Another Hollywood celebrity who clearly ties in Zen Buddhism with martial arts is the well-known actor, Steven Seagal, although he doesn't claim to be a Christian. His Zen spiritual beliefs are noticeable and prevalent in his movies. His martial art of choice is Aikido, which is openly connected to the practice of Zen Buddhism and all that it involves, such as meditation, acupuncture, etc.

When I visited his website, it claimed that if you ask any martial arts expert, they would say that, "It is the spirit that reaches deep within your soul that drives the artistry."[7] We have to ask then, "What is this spirit that drives a person?" My opinion is, it may feel like a *calling*, but is actually more like an *obsession* that drives one to perfect the artistry of the martial arts. Seagal's site said he is "driven to reaching the top of his game in every aspect of life."[8]

Steven Seagal claims to have mastered the martial arts at an early age. He would evolve into becoming what he now claims to be, a 7th degree black belt and Aikido master. (Have you noticed that all of these instructors want and even demand to be called "Master"?) He had, at one time, supposedly trained Sean Connery and James Coburn, as well as other movie actors. However, I find it interesting that much of his mastery and accomplishments are refuted by his Japanese first wife, Miyako Fujitano, as well as others. For more information, you can go to:

http://www.lukeford.net/profiles/profiles/steven_seagal1.htm

In Steven's movies, he is often posing in a meditation position, bowing down to an idol—a statue of Buddha, with incense and flowers all around. His Asian philosophies and religion are not only a way of life, he also proclaims himself to be a Zen Buddhist teacher and healer. He says that he lives by the principle that "development of the physical self is essential to protect the spiritual man."[9] My interpretation of what he is saying is that the spirit that dwells in him has a lot invested in him, and wants to stay there as long as possible, so it has driven him to try to learn self-preservation.

We cannot preserve ourselves even if we wanted to. It is our Creator, God, who gives us the very breath of life we breathe, and it is He who has the right to give life or take it. He alone determines the number of years that we live on this earth. But the influence of an evil spirit would want us to try to usurp God and make us believe we can make our own determination concerning our life and the preservation of it.

Steven's website also stated that, "He believes that what he does in life is about leading people into contemplation to wake them up and enlighten them in some manner."[10] It is okay if we are enlightened and awakened to the truth of God, but there is an enemy of mankind who wants to give us his form of enlightenment, which can either be an outright lie, or a lie packaged in truth. It is usually a lie mixed in with some truth because he knows we would be more likely to identify and reject an outright lie. This is where the subtlety of deception comes in.

Of course, meditation and contemplation of this sort also requires us to "empty our mind." This is the same verbiage one will find in New Age philosophies, in yoga, and TM. I'm sure Steven has many wonderful qualities and he is described as a deeply caring and giving person. He appears to be gentle and sincere, but the spirit in him is not.

In Aikido, the spiritual connection cannot be denied. Those involved claim that the power source—reservoirs of fuel power—reside within the person who is involved. All martial arts and yoga practitioners use the same power, but it is known by different names. As I said earlier, those in the martial arts refer to the power as "ki" or "ch'i," which is a "so-called" universal cosmic energy.

It does come from somewhere, but I can assure you it does not come from God, the Creator of the entire cosmic universe. Nor does it do us good, as many think. This kind of power comes from the spiritual concept and practice of occult meditation, which is behind Hinduism, Buddhism, and Zen. Many actors and actresses are involved in these activities and are probably unaware of the spirits behind them.

I find it interesting how these occult religions use many of the sayings that are in the Bible, such as "silver thread," or "silver cord," or "life force." They call it a universal flow or channeling—a conduit by which they can receive information from an unseen realm. Once again, through these activities, one allows an evil spiritual force to enter—by invitation, I might add!

I remember seeing this flow of energy at a demonstration many years ago when I first became involved in the martial arts. This Aikido demonstration by Koichi Tohei flabbergasted me. I saw him do the "you can't lift me" demonstration. Two huge men were not able to pick him up, unless he let them. Another one was the "unbendable arm," which I learned to do later on, along with a few other things.

But the one that amazed me the most (me, as well as the huge crowd that was in attendance) was when he held a seven-foot staff extended out in front of him and had three or four men try to push the staff and they could not. He then began to push and toss these big guys around like rag dolls. *This is really spooky stuff,* I thought back then. What was making it work? Was it physical human strength alone? No way! I now know what power was really behind these incredible feats of supernatural strength. It was an unseen supernatural force (which is much stronger than human strength) that was operating in and through the willing man, causing him to be able to do extraordinary feats.

There is another actor whom I want to discuss because he, too, has had a tremendous influence on millions of moviegoers. Jean-Claude Van Damme has starred in a number of movies, but his greatest influence came from the movie, "Blood Sport." This movie was a prelude and major contributor to the rise of mixed martial arts that we now see on television, i.e. cage fighting, ultimate fighting, etc. The list is growing and so is the popularity, not to mention the danger. The problem is that as people become more desensitized, they will thirst for more violence, blood, and gore.

There is another so-called sport called "pride fighting." I look at it as well trained, physically conditioned, glorified street fighters who use various aspects of martial arts and boxing together. The spirit behind all of it is violence. Right now, it is all somewhat regulated, but at some point it is going to get out of hand and someone is going to get killed, if they haven't already somewhere around the world.

Entertainment has reached a whole new level here in America. Take wrestling, for example. The participants are all in great physical "steroid" condition. It's what many call entertainment, watching their steroid-enhanced bodies and choreographed moves. If they were actually as strong as they say they are, and they actually hit each other, there wouldn't be too many of them around for long! It is degenerate entertainment, filled with violence.

There is even something out there today called "Submission Wrestling." It is also known as submission fighting, submission grappling, and "No-Gi Jiu Jitsu." It is a combination of wrestling and martial arts techniques. Submission fighting as an element of a larger sport setting is very common in mixed martial arts. Some call it "grappling" and say that it has nothing to do with any martial arts. If it is not accepted in our society in one form, it will be brought in through another form to try to make it palatable and acceptable to anyone and everyone.

In conclusion, I would say it is easy to see how the depiction and presentation of these activities has evolved over the years, and continues to do so. The power, rage, and violence of the unseen forces are becoming more and more evident as it is manifested in their subjects. Hollywood depicts the martial arts experts as able to take on twenty or thirty people at a time and survive. They rise again and again to fight, supposedly undeterred and unscathed. That kind of depiction creates a false illusion of invincibility that has nothing to do with the real world.

Notes

1. From website: "Bruce Lee and Martial Arts: A Christian Perspective" 8 December 2008 http://www.pastornet.net.au/response/articles/135.htm

2. From Wikipedia online, googled "David Carradine" 16 July 2009

3. From Chuck Norris' official website: www.chuckmorris.com 16 June 2008 <http://www.chucknorris.com/html/biog.html>

4. Ibid., 1 June 2008 <http://www.chucknorris.com/html/kick.html>

5. Ibid.

6. Ibid.

7. From Steven Seagal's official website: www.stevenseagal.com 16 June 2008 <http://www.stevenseagal.com/about/>

8. Ibid.

9. Ibid.

10. Ibid.

CHAPTER 4

WEIRD, WACKY, AND DOWNRIGHT DANGEROUS

I WANT TO SHARE FROM PERSONAL experience and observation some of the most bizarre practices, some of which border on insanity. Although I have never directly practiced or became a participant in most of what I am going to describe in the following pages, there are those who have.

I did not understand at the time, nor did I want to know what was really in operation and literally possessing these people, as they demonstrated some of the most spooky, weird, and dangerous exhibitions. I would question in my mind as I observed some really freaky things and I thought, *Where did these people come up with these strange, ludicrous antics that defy good common sense and the laws of physics?* Even when I asked those that had more experience than myself, they did not have a clear understanding either. I would not know the answers until years later, after I was no longer involved—after I was free from all the tentacles of the martial arts in my own life.

I had heard rumors about certain "so-called" chosen people who possessed special mysterious powers in the martial arts, who credited "ki" with their ability to knock a man down by barely touching him, or by merely pointing a finger at him. Some claimed to be able to floor an opponent by their breath, or a look from their eyes. (Others can floor you with their breath simply because they forgot to use mouthwash!)

For years, as I was involved and trained under world-renowned men, not once did any of them even hint to us about this kind of supernatural ability. If anyone knew about it, they would have! In every segment of the martial arts, there are those who seem to go *over the edge.* These are the real "way out" dangerous wackos.

Some of what I am going to describe is scary stuff. When I saw these things, I remember thinking, *Maybe these people have escaped from some kind of institution for the mentally challenged.* These people were "way out there." And yet thousands of people view these individuals as they demonstrate their abilities and skills via the Internet, movies, television, public forums, etc., and think nothing of it!

The reason these people perform some of these things is to impress the viewers with their physical abilities and knowledge that they apparently believe puts them in a category far above everyone else. They want to be called "masters," desiring to be exalted because of their great skills (that only they possess) or that were passed on to them by other masters—kind of a *family thing.* Actually that really is the case, but the master who passed it along and endowed them with this so-called knowledge is their unseen master of deception, who empowers them and makes what they do apparently work. That is what I always wondered, *What makes it work?*

I have described in earlier chapters the connection between the physical realm and the unseen spiritual realm. There is a direct connection between the religions of Hinduism, Buddhism, and Zen, and the meditation and communication lines, which were established in the spirit realm within these religions. As I have emphatically stated, what came out of this meditation and communication with the spirit realm was what actually gave birth to the martial arts in the first place. It came through yoga! (Remember the picture of the man in a karate uniform sitting in a yoga "lotus" position? A picture is worth a thousand words!)

The religious gurus (the enlightened ones, as they were called by their followers) know it is impossible to separate the spiritual roots from the physical, and that the crossover from one to the other is but a breath away. And that is exactly what it takes—breathing, exercising, and meditation. It is all intricately tied together—breathing, spirit, focus...body, mind, spirit coordination.

It is what the people who practice these religions call their access to a universal flow of (or transfer of) information, and everything else that operates in the *dark side* of this universe. Remember the dark side in "Star Wars," which opposed the *light side?* In other words, through this practice, people become channels or conduits. It is warmed-over Hinduism—New Age practices—that have been westernized!

When one aligns the body and the spirit, focusing intently through certain breathing exercises, one opens oneself up to the "ki" or "ch'i" or "prana" powers, no matter what form it is done in, whether it is Karate, Tae Kwon Do, Kung Fu, Jujitsu, Aikido, Tai Ch'i Chuan, or yoga, etc. They all gain their power from the supposed reservoir that connects the spirit realm and the physical realm. At that point, the channel (or conduit) is open to all, no matter the depth of participation, how long one is involved, or what label it is done under.

Unfortunately, those who practice or become involved in some form or another believe, or at least are told, that one can separate the spiritual from the physical by adding or deleting some element—that it is safe and has nothing to do with eastern religions. Denial and/or deception take its toll. The instructors are deceived. How can those who believe them not also be deceived? *Why would they even mention that one can separate the two, if they weren't very concerned that someone might discover there really is a strong connection?* The reason is simple. Inwardly, they know the truth, but they will do their best to keep it hidden from you!

This is the big lie and it opens wide the door, bringing a massive mountain of deception into one's life. Whatever we decide to come into agreement with, we are, in essence, accepting the consequences that come with it. It is part of the package. There is a very clear and present danger that will eventually affect those who are involved in various adverse ways that can be far-reaching.

The consequences of involvement, as I have experienced in my own life, and have seen in many others, can be spiritual blindness, immorality, fear, pride, anger, and the inability to have understanding and make good, sound choices. If people who have been involved want to be completely free from these adverse effects, they will need to go through a process of deliverance (spiritually speaking).

However, those who choose to remain and go deeper in their involvement will find that as they continue to give themselves over to the spiritual powers that are at work, they will be under a firmly-entrenched spiritual stronghold. Those who choose to continue to give these spirits unhindered ability to operate in and through them (controlling many areas of their soulish realm and physical body) will suffer the consequences.

There is always some level of behavioral modification that will eventually come to fruition and it will manifest in different ways in the physical realm. One result will be a noticeable change in that person's personality. When I was training as a student in Chicago, Illinois, my instructor, Mr. Sugiyama, was a very skilled, extremely strong man. He had what is known as *"the way of the warrior"*— the Bushido spirit. I wanted to be like him and have the same spirit. Well, I got that spirit, and a whole lot more to go with it, even though I did not practice meditation, except to kneel, *clear my mind*, and bow down to the instructor or other students before and after each class. *That was harmless enough*—I thought!

Although Mr. Sugiyama practiced Shinto and Zen, he never talked about, taught, or pushed his religious practices. But it didn't make any difference. Just the involvement and the physical aspect of submitting to the practice of Karate (the way it was taught) were enough. The transfer was covert. The breathing exercises, the clearing of the mind, and the flow of what we were doing physically were enough to open the door to my soul, even if I had not bowed to my instructor. It was all transferred even though I did not practice any religious requirements for becoming a Zen Buddhist. It is all cleverly incorporated into the training itself.

There was a definitive transfer of a power that propelled me forward to become what I became—just like him! The flow from that universal or cosmic spiritual power zapped me and at that point I became like Dr. Jekyll and Mr. Hyde. I would turn on and off like flipping a light switch—manifesting extreme opposites in personality.

During my earlier years of Karate exhibitions, I was able to do some pretty amazing things, or so I thought at the time. For example, I was able to do something which was known as the "unbendable arm." I would place my arm (palm up) on a person's shoulder and that same person, using his full weight, would put both his arms on mine and try to bend my arm, but he couldn't.

I also did something known as the one-inch punch. I didn't understand exactly how it worked at the time. I would put pads on a person's chest, hold my fist one inch away, and without drawing back I would hit that person from one inch away, either knocking the breath out of them, or knocking them down. I was also able to break stacks of concrete blocks with a single blow of my hand. It was relatively easy for me to do that—without any pain or injury—at the time. (However, the cumulative damaging effects caught up with me later.)

At some point, I recognized that in my own physical strength I could never have done most of these things. It wasn't until I began to advance that I realized there had to be something much greater than just my own physical strength that was enabling me to do these feats. At the time, however, even as I progressed in these activities, I had only a veiled understanding of the source of power that I had inadvertently allowed to grow and operate in and through my life.

It was this demonic flow of power (called "ki") that I had allowed to reside in me. The more I trained, the stronger that power became! That power took up residence in my lower abdomen (called the tandem area) a few inches below my navel. The belly button is the lifeline that a baby needs to connect in order to survive in the natural womb. So the same is true with the spiritual connection. That powerful engine in my lower stomach was where the power resided and flowed to and from every part of my body, and beyond, as I participated in these activities.

On the contrary, if one is a Christian, one knows the Bible says in John 7:38 (KJV) that if we are filled with the power of God that out of our bellies will "flow rivers of living water." The resultant effect will be to refresh those around us—bringing truth, power, wisdom, peace, and love to all who are touched by these "rivers." The power I had back then was the diametric opposite of God's power.

It takes fuel to run a power plant to generate electricity; it takes fuel to run an engine, to make it do whatever it is designed to do. I can assure you from my own experience that without help from the spiritual demonic realm, which provides the spiritual power source, those involved in martial arts and related practices will not be able to use the arts for which they were designed, using just their physical strength alone. But all who become involved in martial arts and yoga, to any degree, open themselves up to the power from that same evil spiritual realm. *That is the nature of the beast of these eastern practices.*

As I have said before, there are those who are already involved who try to convince (and often do) that these eastern arts are pure and innocent and are simply for sport, self-defense, health benefits, and/or confidence building. These proponents will say these arts are no different than western sports such as baseball, football, tennis, golf, etc. But I remind you, these western sports activities were not developed from eastern religions which are deeply rooted in the occult. I repeat this here to make it clear that other sports do not depend on the drawing of physical power by accessing the spirit realm through eastern practices of meditation and other techniques, which are inherent in the training.

Although I was heavily involved in Shotokan Karate for years, I did not get involved directly in the really bizarre aspects that so many have become involved in. Some of the things I learned—such as the "you can't bend my arm thing" or "you can't pick me up thing" were not techniques that took hours of instruction to learn. They just seemed to come naturally as I progressed.

Over the years, I have seen and heard some really bizarre things. Some were exaggerated and some were myths, but not all. For example,

Mr. Tsutomu Ohshima, a high-level instructor (a Japanese native who was also trained in Shotokan Karate) had developed some techniques that would scare the pants off most people, including me. I had seen some weird things, but nothing like I was about to see on one particular day.

He used to teach about the color and shape of one's eyes. He taught that if you could see the whole eyeball as all white, it meant in Japan that one was a murderer. He also said that the one who had an all-white eyeball also had the ability to change the entire white area where it would become almost completely black. By doing this, that person would be able to totally control another person. Does that sound impossible, unbelievable, and far-fetched?

Mr. Ohshima did develop the ability to dilate his eyes (or so he said) so that they became black, as he had shared that murderers do in Japan. Why? That was my reaction. Why would he want to turn the whites of his eyes all black? Why place himself in the same category as a murderer? Why teach something so bizarre? I believe the answer is that what was operating in him gave him that ability to do so. Secondly, it was for control purposes, to intimidate and scare the other person, and to exalt himself as someone special. I believe that the eyes are the windows to one's soul, and Mr. Ohshima blatantly revealed what was operating in and through him.

You are probably saying by now, "Come on, Vito, that's not possible – that is too weird!" But, "Seeing is believing," some say. Let me give you an example. A few years ago, I had a construction business. One day I went to the site to check on the progress of a particular project to see how my men were doing. The owner was there, along with her son who was about fourteen years old, and her daughter, who was about twelve. I knew the son was into some weird stuff, but I didn't know much about the daughter.

I happened to come onto the site as an argument was ensuing between the girl and her mother about something the girl wanted to do, and the mother was disagreeing with her. I was standing about five feet away, waiting for the argument to end, so I could discuss some work-related details. Well, lo and behold, right in front of me a transformation took place in the girl. Suddenly, the eyes—I mean all of both her eyes—turned totally black and the girl snarled at her mother, who began to tremble with fear. She half covered her face with her hands and began to shake, as the power in this girl seemed to take complete control over the mother. I watched as the mother backed away, gave in, and said, "Do whatever you want!" Within about a minute, the girl's eyes returned back to normal.

Although I wasn't there when the argument started, I certainly saw the final outcome. *There was a demon in operation, like that in Mr. Ohshima, which manifested in order to control another person.* I instinctively recognized what was in operation and knew how to set this girl free, but I did not have the permission of the mother to use my authority to cast the demon out. Besides, it had a legal right to be there, so even if I had cast it out, it would have come right back. It was not directed at me, but at the mother, who was the authority in this particular situation. If the intimidation tactic had been directed at me personally, I would have bound it up and forbidden it to continue to operate against me.

I did not intervene or try to stop what was manifesting through this girl because this was a family issue that had been ongoing for many years in their home. I did know what to do and I could have stopped it. But it would have been futile to cast it out as long as the family members were not Christian, and the mother kept giving in to the daughter on these kinds of issues.

The mother later told me that she feared for her life at times, and that this kind of situation had happened many times before. She didn't know how to explain it or how to deal with it. By the way, both of her children had been in Karate. Over the years, I have seen similar manifestations in both students and instructors (in the martial arts) who exhibited demonic control, but none quite this extreme.

Many times I have seen strange things operating in those involved in martial arts, such as extreme uncontrollable violence, coming from nowhere, in people who (to my knowledge) had never before exhibited that kind of behavior. I have seen strange facial contortions (like Bruce Lee and his "wannabes") or totally blank expressions on their faces, as if their minds were completely gone. I believe they were taken over, at least temporarily. Also, I have heard screams that were out of control. It wasn't until I was free from the strongholds of martial arts spirits that I would understand the truth and see what was in operation (spiritually) to cause all these bizarre manifestations.

Many people are gullible, to say the least, and are mesmerized by the reputation and high-level skills of many of these so-called masters. People in these arts have strong tendencies to believe everything their masters and gurus tell them. Oftentimes, the students perceive their instructors as *larger than life*, which only adds to the myths and reputations of these people, making them seem as "gods" in the eyes of many.

Practitioners idolize them, and in many cases worship them, hoping they will impart some special gift to them. (They will, but what they get may not be what they want!) I admit that I was guilty when I was impressed by certain high-level instructors, but it didn't last very long when I became knowledgeable in the Lord Jesus Christ and began to see through the façade.

I have experienced times when these masters would enter a dojo and everyone would begin to acknowledge their presence, their status, and reputation by immediately stopping whatever they were doing and bowing to them. At times, people would reverence them as if they were some kind of holy men. The atmosphere would actually change when that happened. This is nothing short of idolatry.

In every club or program where the martial arts or yoga are practiced (whether in a dojo, YMCA, school, church, or a gym) one can discern, even tangibly feel, that there is an uneasiness of some sort. Many times, one can sense violence or pride immediately. Sometimes it feels so evil that it makes one's skin crawl or the hair on the back of the neck to rise. Most people ignore what they are feeling and, thereby, become desensitized over time!

> *Most people ignore what they are feeling and, thereby, become desensitized over time!*

They know that something is in the air, but they can't explain it, and may come to believe that it is their own imagination. It is that "so-called" cosmic flow or energy, but one does not have to be in a dojo to feel it. One can feel it by just being around people who are involved.

The higher and deeper instructors were in their field of expertise, the greater the energy level. One could feel the presence and the power that emanated from them. It wasn't reverence, but fear—fear of what was operating in that so-called master. It was so intense and formidable, that whatever that person commanded one to do, people would do without thinking twice! There was a high degree of control and manipulation. It is unadulterated idol worship—which is what the gurus and senseis want. Bow down to them and they will reward you for it. Yes, but what kind of reward?

In the Asian culture, bowing is a way of greeting and showing honor and respect. In the West, we shake hands when we meet or greet someone. But bowing in martial arts takes on an entirely different meaning. It can mean a greeting, but most often it is an act of total unquestioning submission to the other person, especially when one is bowing to an instructor. (Students also bow to each other and to those other students who are superior in rank.) It is a mechanical gesture—yet it has a greater significance.

There were times when I had new students who expressed to me that they had a sense of uneasiness about bowing to me or to the other students. I would always say something like this: "It's only showing respect," or "It's like a handshake." But actually that is not totally true. It is also a spiritual gesture. When two martial arts students bow to each other before a match, it is a challenge. The spirit in the one is challenging the spirit in the other. Remember, the match is not a meeting to have a friendly conversation or get to know one another. It's combat. When else would we shake hands or show respect when violent confrontation is about to take place?

Also, bowing to the master in front of the class or to a picture of a dead master is not showing respect. It is showing adulation (or worship) to a superior spirit that inhabits (or inhabited the instructor if he is deceased). It makes no difference whether one is bowing while sitting on the floor, or while standing, the intent is still the same. It is a religious Zen practice that I had done without thinking twice—thousands of times—with no understanding of what I was actually doing.

Hindus, Buddhists, and Zen Buddhists all bow to each other, palms together. This is a type of body language you will see when you travel to other parts of the world. What are they saying without actually saying it? *"The god in me acknowledges the god in you!"* I know there is a saying that, "When in Rome, do as the Romans do." But as Westerners, especially if one is a Christian, we should not be so quick to do anything and everything we see others do, without knowing the spiritual significance behind it.

Nothing that I have experienced will come close to comparing with what I am about to share. Over the years, some really whacked out and very dangerous people have emerged doing such bizarre things that are so insane that it makes what I have discussed so far seem like "child's play."

The Death Yell

Throughout history, we find that armies, which were about to engage in a battle, were taught to yell as loudly as they could when attacking their enemy. It was done for several reasons. It does have a purpose. First of all, it was done to stir up the natural adrenaline to give an increase in strength, and secondly, it was done to put the fear of them into the enemy. It was also done to help stem the fear in the one doing the attacking, taking one's mind off the impending battle, which they fully knew could result in their injury or even death.

The yelling can often intimidate the other person. It sounds reasonable and it works. You will also hear yelling in football, weight lifting, and other sports, all for the purpose of gaining the upper hand, if they can. It is an adrenaline rush that people get in doing a lot of these things.

But this kind of yelling is not the same as it is in the martial arts. In the martial arts, it's called the "kiai", and the yell that comes forth is designed to focus all attention on a particular point on a real or imagined person. The goal is two-fold:

1. To have enough intensity to penetrate the psyche of the mind for the purpose of weakening their opponent's defense.

2. To focus on the exact point where contact is to be made. This happens, especially in "kata," which is a series of choreographed moves that martial artists do when defending or attacking an imaginary opponent. Imaginary opponent – imagine that!

It is called "controlled violence" and is done in such a way that the opponent is not injured. (At least that is the intent, but is not always the case.) The "kiai" at times is so strong that it can startle the people in the dojo, even vibrating windows at times. That's powerful! But I have never seen a "kiai" (yell) hurt anyone physically. Not even from the very best of yellers! The most I ever heard of was the one yelling got a headache or strained vocal cords. What I am about to tell you is an example of an extreme demonstration of the "so-called" death yell.

Imaginary opponent – imagine that!

One Saturday afternoon a couple of years ago, I turned on the television looking for a decent program to watch. While I was surfing through the channels, I came to what I believe was the Discovery channel, which usually has some pretty interesting and informational programs. But this one was over the top. There was a weird-looking man dressed in a Karate uniform, but he didn't speak very good English, so I assumed he came from another country. After watching him for a few minutes, I came to a quick conclusion that he was so far out he must have been from Pluto or some other planet.

This man, whom I called a "master of disaster," claimed he had developed what he called *the death yell*. He went on to say that through his special techniques, he could stop an aggressor in his tracks, without touching him—using only his special yell, or "kiai". He claimed the sound that he emitted (audible, of course) could not be seen. (When can anybody see sound?) He claimed to be able not only to stop a person, but also totally disable him, even kill. He had some students assisting him who were from the same "planet" he was from (I think). They were all part of this mindless, sound thing.

He went on to say he could use his "kiai" yell to even ring a bell from various distances. (I think he had bells in his head.) The claims that came out of his mouth became more and more exaggerated the longer he talked, especially when he began to claim that he had killed birds in flight with a single yell. He did say, however, that he would never use his skills to harm or kill a human being. I wasn't sure if I trusted the integrity of that statement.

As I watched this man, there were several things I noted. First of all, the students who were assisting him did not seem to be too bright. They seemed to be rather distant or spaced out. Secondly, if this man's claims were even slightly true, how much of this super power was he able to harness? I wondered, *What if there was too much of this secret power released in the presence of people? Would it not harm them, if he could kill a bird and ring a bell, or stop a person in his tracks? How did he know it wouldn't kill a human? Had he ever come close?* I saw that his students were like puppets under his control. By his so-called death yell, he was able to knock down his "mind-controlled" students on command.

If all these weird and wacky methods were possible, what would their purpose be? Would it be only for a select few masters and gurus? I wonder if he could teach our soldiers to use his methods to disable or kill the enemy in combat, or maybe teach law enforcement officers to use yelling to disable a person who might be behind the door (where they could not taser them). This would surely save lives and a lot of bullets in the heat of the battle. Perhaps he could use a loud speaker long distance and drop the enemy without putting himself in harm's way. (I'm kidding, of course.)

People could save all that money they pour out for training long hours in the gym; instead everyone could learn to yell. There would be no need for physical exercise. One could just *will* his body into shape and then he could spend more time with family and friends. There would be no lengthy hours of training with these talented masters and gurus who could instead teach everyone mind control. Isn't that what it is anyway?

What is behind the so-called "inner consciousness movement," not only in martial arts, but also in yoga? It is mind control, which equates to deception and spiritual control. There are different functions, different names, and different levels, but all are rooted in the same source of cosmic demonic power.

A bizarre story I found on the Internet when I googled "death touch" told of a man who claimed he could affect the nervous system of people by yelling at them without touching them. He was called *the human stun gun*. Investigative reporters watched him use his "so-called" energy to knock his students down, paralyzing their nervous systems, and then he supposedly used his power to restore them. However, when he tried to use the same power on the reporter, he failed miserably. *The reason it only worked on his students is because they had chosen to subject themselves to come under his influence and power.* In the end, the reporter declared him to be a fake and a fraud.

I also saw on a number of occasions this yelling thing come forth from instructors whose only expertise seemed to be yelling as loud as they could to try to intimidate or impress their students, or intimidate others who were watching and impress them with how much power they possessed. The louder, the more power, or so they thought. This yelling thing is widespread in the martial arts.

One of my former students (I will call him Robert) was a nice enough young man, but he was not consistent in his training and consequently didn't develop much talent (physically) in Karate. I trained him off and on for about twelve months. A couple of years later (after I became a Christian) I left the martial arts scene. But he came back on the scene, suddenly with all this knowledge and rank. When he was with me, his training was sparse and the Japanese instructor who came to my dojo did not like him, for whatever reason. Once, in Chicago during a test, the Japanese instructor yelled at him, told him to get dressed, leave the dojo, and never come back. Now that's a yell that worked!

They did not like his attitude, nor did they like the way he was self-training and trying to elevate and promote himself, without going through the basic hard work and discipline required for a legitimate belt ranking. By the spirits operating in them, they knew the short cuts he was trying to take to become somebody of rank and status, without the hard work!

A few years later, he developed a website, which claims that he is one of the most prolific writers on the subject of martial arts. But from my experience, I can tell you it could be very dangerous to be trained or taught by anyone who has been "self taught." But whether it is more dangerous than being trained by an expert—well, you decide. It's a dangerous activity, either way.

I remember a couple of times I passed by his dojo (which moved about every six months or so). One day I decided to surprise him and stop by unannounced to say hello. When he saw me, he panicked. Before he saw me, his voice was normal and he was barking out a few commands. But when he saw me, his barking became yells and screams. I believe he thought I was there to expose him and his superficial sixth or seventh-degree ranking, which would have been embarrassing in front of his students. I didn't, and it wasn't my intent, but his students were very startled by his sudden outburst, to say the least. I believe he was yelling to try to cover his fear, and at the same time trying to intimidate me and, hopefully, scare me away. Needless to say, it didn't work.

It was years later, after that interesting encounter in the dojo, that I heard that he had had a heart attack and was in intensive care in the hospital. (By that time, he knew I had become a Christian.) I paid him a visit because he was in bad shape and I asked him if he would like me to pray for him. He had come from a good Christian home, so I knew he understood. He agreed and seemed grateful for prayer.

He was miraculously healed by God through that prayer, but six months later someone showed me an article in Black Belt Magazine that had this headline: *Man With Fatal Heart Attack Attributes his Healing to the Martial Arts* "Karate." The article was about this same man. There was no mention of prayer, God, or even doctors—only the spiritual forces that were empowering him and causing him to believe that he was healed by them. It was God who healed him, but he failed to acknowledge it.

The Death Touch

Another of the *far out* elaborated martial arts concepts is the mysterious "so-called" death touch. This is a cousin to the death yell! This particular secret form has a few different names. In Cantonese (Chinese) it is called dim mak, and in Japanese, Kyusho Jitsu (which means "the touch of death"). The death yell and the death touch are related to each other in much the same way as the evil twins of acupuncture and acupressure.

The idea (at least in many people's minds) is that a touch or squeeze applied to certain pressure points will *supposedly* cause the victim's "ch'i" (or energy) to be rendered paralyzed or incapacitated, resulting in their possible death. (The practitioners claim that this "ch'i" flows through the body along certain lines which they call meridians.) There are those who claim to have these abilities, to cause death by their touch. Spock, on the television series "Star Trek," was portrayed to have this ability that no one else on the show had. He was a Vulcan, so maybe only Vulcans have that ability!

I was surprised recently by a nationally-aired program called Real TV in which they were advertising the death touch. After years of hearing about this so-called "death touch," I was curious about exactly how this was going to be played out on national television, so I watched it. There are those who seem to thrive on the weird and ridiculous. In order to get the spirit that gives one the ability to perform these unsubstantiated feats, one must be trained and indoctrinated in the (you guessed it) martial arts. Do you get the connection?

The TV program began by showing a man dressed in a Karate uniform. From his appearance he looked to be more than a little out of shape. He was standing with five or six students who were surrounding him in a circle. His demonstration was designed to impress people with his ability to take life—and then give it back. He went on to explain that what he was about to do was very dangerous and should not be tried at home. *Oh, duh*, I thought, *how could anyone apply a death touch with no knowledge of how to do it?*

As he began, his students foolishly submitted to having this man (in the middle of his madness) strike them with various touches on their bodies. I think the students were suffering from what most people involved in these crazy escapades suffer from – M.D.S. (Mental Deterioration Syndrome). The media crew was filming from every direction to capture the essence of this exhibition so the viewing audience would not miss the excitement.

Paramedic crews with resuscitation equipment surrounded the area, and ambulances waited outside in case of an emergency! As the students were struck, they began to fall like bowling pins, paralyzed and supposedly close to death from the touch of their crazed master. Then, with swiftness, he went from student to student and touched them and they miraculously recovered. The medical crews were only there in the event that this guy failed to do what he claimed, or was not able to revive these students who were suffering from M.D.S. This kind of thing leaves a lot of unanswered questions.

Food for Thought

1. Who in their right mind would willingly let anyone strike them with a potential deathblow? Yet all did.

2. If it was so dangerous, why would anyone with a sane mind become a guinea pig so another person would look like he had great mystical powers?

3. It is still illegal to kill or seriously injure a person unless it is done in self-defense, where one's life may be in danger.

4. It is obvious that there must have been practice sessions before these techniques were performed in front of a live audience or how else would they know that they would work? Were medical crews and ambulances standing by then?

5. Why call it a death touch when no one died? Why not call it a "knock-out" touch, or some other name? The answer is clear. It is all about show-manship, sensationalism, and control from these masters who yearn to be idolized by students and observers alike.

6. Hitting a stationary target is one thing; hitting a moving one is another story. In real life, no one is likely to be standing perfectly still allowing another person to do whatever he might want to do.

Another bizarre concept that has been perpetuated in the martial arts circles is that certain "so-called" masters have the ability to reach into a man's body and pull out his still-beating heart, while the man is look-ing at him, and then goes into shock and dies. Interestingly, in the third Indiana Jones movie, "The Temple of Doom," Indiana Jones is facing a shaman who does just that—to another man—as Jones looks on.

The evil Indian shaman who performed this act of removing the man's heart supposedly does it somewhere in India in a cave, where hundreds of young children were kept "under a spell" of forced labor, working in the mines. This evil shaman (Hindu witch doctor) did not use any martial arts' techniques, but yet this myth is perpetuated both in martial arts and in the occult. There seems to be a lot of overlapping here, wouldn't you say?

Ninjas

The most famous (or should I say infamous) users of "so-called" special powers were the Ninjas from Japan, hence the Ninja death touch. Most people do not know their origin or real purpose. The Ninjas were paid assassins, the worst of the worst, and more dangerous and violent than anyone can imagine. Their sole purpose was to kill often innocent people by stealth, poison, or some other means. They would be akin to today's "for hire" hit men.

Recently in Florida, a group of men attacked a very wealthy couple who had sixteen children (many of them adopted, and some with special needs). It was captured on a security camera and also reported that several men (dressed in Ninja garb) invaded the home and attacked with such military-style precision and efficiency that it was dubbed "a Ninja-style killing." One thing I found interesting was that one of the men arrested and believed to be one of those who planned the attack and murder was a martial arts instructor who taught children self-defense.

Nin Jitsu means "the art of stealth," and is said to have originated between 593 and 628 A.D. Ninjas (those who practice Nin Jitsu) were typically "warrior-mystics" in the mountainous regions of south central Japan. They lived and trained in Buddhist monasteries. They were often contracted by Japan's professional warriors (none of whom generally practiced Nin Jitsu themselves) to engage in espionage, sabotage, and murder.

Nin Jitsu is still practiced today as a martial art. Oftentimes, in movies especially, one can see their appearance with black outfits (including black hoods) operating in secret assignments, using all forms of weapons to eliminate all opposition. Their assignment is simple—death by any means.

Today, these same assassins are glamorized on television, in movies, and incredibly made out to be the *good guys*, even in children's movies, video games, and toys such as Ninja turtles. How can a turtle, of all things, be a Ninja? They are subtly marketed, along with a host of other demonically-influenced things that are designed to adversely affect our children, all the while desensitizing them to the violence which they represent! For example, there are the Teenage Mutant Ninja Turtles—four pizza-eating, surf-talking, life-sized turtles—whose movies, cartoons, toys, and snacks have translated into incredible profits, some $500 million per year!

All these martial arts items are cleverly disguised and packaged, the most recent being the Kung Fu Panda movie, which has gained much popularity among children and adults alike. What does a cute Chinese panda have to do with Kung Fu, other than the fact that they are both from China? There have been monumental efforts to sanitize these ancient fighting arts by connecting them with adorable and innocent pets.

CHAPTER 5

KIDS IN KARATE

DO YOU REMEMBER THE MOVIE "The Karate Kid"? It made its debut in 1984 and became a hit movie. It starred a young man who moved from New Jersey to a California town with his mother. They moved into an apartment complex where there was a Japanese-American handyman who was the maintenance man for the complex.

The young man was a good kid. He began to meet people and he met a young girl whose ex-boyfriend was heavily involved in the martial arts. The ex-boyfriend started an argument with his ex-girlfriend and ended up pushing her, in his anger. The kid himself had had a few lessons in martial arts back in New Jersey, so he jumps in and tries to defend the girl. The fight escalated and the ex-boyfriend becomes even more upset, jealous, and violent—beating up the innocent new kid who simply wanted to enjoy a nice day, making friends on the beach. It would get worse before it got better!

A few days later, after the kid (whose name was Daniel) had continued to befriend the ex-girlfriend, the ex-boyfriend became really jealous. In a jealous rage, he proceeded to beat Daniel up pretty badly, leaving him with a huge black eye. The young teen who beat the new kid up had trained for some time in the martial arts and had become accomplished enough to be a well-trained black belt.

In theory, that kind of training is to learn self-defense, self-control, self-confidence, and to become physically fit. That means, theoretically, that as a student in martial arts he should have been disciplined enough to diffuse the situation. He should have been able to control his anger enough to avoid conflict, especially when he sensed the new kid knew relatively nothing as far as how to defend himself. But that wasn't the case.

That theory is a fallacy and even though this was "just a movie," this type of behavior is fairly typical in situations similar to the movie. The teenage black belt was emulating his instructor to a tee. His instructor had passed on his own hate, violence, and the lack of control to his students. I cannot even count the number of times I have witnessed the same behavior coming from very similar instructors in dojos all across America.

If you have not seen the movie, I am not suggesting you go out and rent it, but if you have, you will get the point. The new kid on the block, who just got beat up, subsequently meets the Japanese handyman in the complex where he lives. The handyman turns out to be a secret martial arts expert who offers to train young Daniel when he spots his huge black eye. But his training methods must have come from another universe or something! The handyman expert, whose name is Mr. Miyagi, starts the training by having Daniel wax his cars. The kid is instructed to "put the wax on and take the wax off." Wise Mr. Miyagi gets his cars waxed and polished and the kid only gets sore muscles.

But the kid believes that the training methods (which later included such things as standing on one leg, flapping his arms like a whooping crane, and some other weird things) will be sufficient enough for him to learn to defend himself against a well-trained black belt. He also learns how to do strange things like catching a common housefly in mid air with a pair of chopsticks, which he is able to do after only a few tries. (Even his instructor who had tried for years had not been able to do that.)

His continual instruction to Daniel was, "Focus, concentrate, concentrate, focus!" After this period of very strange training, Mr. Miyagi goes on to make a deal with the teenager's sensei. The deal he made was that the well-trained black belt would not continue to pick on young Daniel-san as he had been doing, but rather that the dispute should be settled in the ring once for all.

The time comes after a few months of "wax on, wax off" training for Daniel to use his newfound skills to enter an open Karate tournament to settle the dispute. He is greatly encouraged by Mr. Miyagi, who hands him a black belt and enters him against well-seasoned black belts who have been trained for years for competition. Amazingly, Daniel goes on to win the competition against unbelievable odds. Only in Hollywood would that be possible.

I would say to you what Mr. Miyagi said to Daniel, "Focus and concentrate on what I am about to tell you." As a word of caution to parents everywhere, when you enroll your kids (or yourself) in martial arts classes, you are throwing caution to the wind and there will be a reaping of an evil harvest from any involvement in the martial arts. It will be more than just catching a fly with chopsticks! The harvest I'm talking about (what will eventually manifest on the surface) is indicative of seeds that have been planted in that person's life. It may not show up for many years, but it can and will manifest in many different ways and may grow in intensity.

The Fear Factor

There is a strategic plan today that is targeting children more than ever—the younger, the better—many as young as two or three. Karate and Tae Kwon Do clubs are on the increase, and so is the push to get the kids enrolled. By the way, in some places they are now called names such as "Tae Kwon Do University." The advertisements and methods of promotion vary from place to place.

The YMCA claims they are a Christian organization, yet they have unwittingly (and probably unknowingly) allowed many occult activities in their facilities—programs such as martial arts, yoga, and transcendental meditation. Their thrust of advertising includes, "family fitness, family fun, exercise, and physical fitness for all ages." It's all about the money!

The movie "The Karate Kid" was hugely instrumental in helping promote the ideas of self-defense, self-confidence, and self-discipline. But there are also many other promotional methods being used to encourage parents to enroll their kids in martial arts. The underlying goal of these promotional concepts may be to encourage parents to keep their kids from being the next victim on the six o'clock news. Or it may be to protect them from the school bully, or worse yet, assault or kidnapping by a complete stranger. The fears of parents and children alike have certainly been a huge factor in the increased enrollment in various kinds of self-defense classes.

I understand these fears. Years ago, I myself wanted to promote the teaching of self-defense techniques for that very reason, using the vast experience that I had. At the time, I developed a 30-minute film called, "More Than a Fighting Chance," hoping to accomplish that goal. Now, I thank God that it never really got off the ground and you will understand why by the time you finish this book!

Because of these fears, many parents have already enrolled their kids in Karate, Tae Kwon Do or some other form of martial arts (some of which I can't even pronounce). What is often not known up front is exactly what these classes will entail. It will not be like the innocent-looking training methods in "The Karate Kid" of "wax on, wax off," standing on one leg looking like a crane, and an easy road to getting a black belt. It will involve a lot of grueling training.

Most probably there will also be the transfer of more than just physical knowledge—they will receive dangerous spiritual powers as well. When one opens oneself up to the spiritual powers, these hidden forces potentially now have full access. Spiritual seeds are thus planted into the lives of innocent men, women, and children that can affect them in ways that may not show up until much later in life. By then, the seed has germinated and taken root in that person's life. Not everyone who participates is a candidate for these things, but it will affect most people adversely in one way or another.

Let me say here that many parents also allow their children to entertain themselves for hours on end by looking at and participating in certain video games, many of which are quite violent. Perhaps it keeps the children out of trouble and out of their hair, so they allow them to do whatever they want, and maybe never monitor the content of what they are actually watching. It might be because all their friends are doing it and they yield to the pressure from their children.

I don't know all the reasons, but I do know this is a troubling scenario. The problem is, the trouble they may think they are keeping them out of may manifest instead in another area of that child's life (or personality) because of the negative influence from the violence on the video games. Obviously, these things are also influencing teenagers and young adults as well.

The DNA of evil is that it is always looking for and snaring its victims at earlier and earlier stages in their innocent lives and will use whatever method(s) it can to accomplish its goal. Through many electronic devices, games, movies, and other activities, we, as a society, have opened the door and actually aided the enemy of mankind by unconsciously inviting him into our very living rooms. When violence takes a front seat in a person's life and is accepted as "par for the course," then the forces that perpetuate violence are succeeding. When we stand and do nothing, then we are guilty of compromise and passivity.

Will we eventually make the connection between "cause and effect?" Will it be when we begin to see an entire generation of young people who are influenced by fantasies, which often become a reality when they find themselves controlled by forces of violence? Unless we do something about it, this trend will continue generation after generation until a vast harvest of violence is produced and we are reaping the whirlwind, wondering, *How on earth did we get to this place?* One of the problems is that we often do not realize we are captured until it's almost too late. Then we need help getting free, or unstuck.

The movie, "The Karate Kid," showed the good, the bad, the ugly, and the ridiculous. After the movie came out, parents were saying, "My kids could use this Karate training," whether they needed it or not. Kids were begging their parents to let them learn Karate. Neither the parents nor the children understood the spiritual ramifications.

Yet they dove in blindly, not knowing about what was just under the surface—the dangerous seeds of violence, pride, anger, and invincibility that would be planted in the fertile ground of young, innocent lives. Because these kids subject (and submit) themselves to their instructors, and because of his background, these seeds are imparted—mentally, physically, and spiritually—through the "laying on of hands" by the instructors. A transference takes place.

Parents are often comforted by the false perception that sending little Johnny or Susie to a self-defense class might give them a clear advantage over a would-be attacker. *But self-defense as a primary reason to become involved in martial arts is not a good enough reason.* Experts say (and statistics prove) that children would be better off to run, scream, or cause a commotion, rather than stand in their little Karate stance trying to look mean or scare off the attacker. This rarely works because there are so many unknowns and variables, such as when weapons might be involved.

Out on the street would not be a *controlled environment*, such as the practice dojo where they know what to expect from their fellow students and their instructors. Doubt and fear could, and probably would, overtake them. Practicing in a gym is a whole lot different than what can happen on the street where there might also be multiple attackers involved, or all sorts of weapons. Can a child of six, seven, or even ten really defend him or herself against a determined, violent adult attacker, one who is possibly armed with a weapon? Children can have all the little black belts one can earn and still not be equipped to defend themselves adequately.

After-school Karate programs are on the rise. Many clubs are finding it very profitable to offer to even pick kids up after school. Wow, what a novel idea! Now all the other kids get to see little Johnny picked up in the van that says "After-school Karate Classes," painted all over it. Now they all know what Johnny does after school. Oops...there goes the element of surprise! The school bully can read too, you know! The question is, "Will he provoke Johnny to see just how much he has learned?" There goes the "advantage," if there ever was one.

There is hardly a week that goes by that my wife and I do not see five and six-year olds with their little Karate uniforms on and their various colored belts wrapped around them. We see them in malls, restaurants, or just walking the streets. They are "walking displays" of what they do! I remember the time when it was not allowed to wear one's uniform outside the dojo. Today, it is considered good advertisement. Many of the kids who see them are begging or nagging their parents to enroll them in Karate classes so they can be like all their friends. These classes involve contracts and money that could be spent in much more beneficial ways.

A few years ago, I attended a church service with a friend of mine. He introduced me to an instructor who had been allowed to conduct Karate classes for kids in the church he attended. This instructor tried his best to convince me that there was nothing wrong with teaching kids Karate, and how he had made it "safe, acceptable, and compatible with Christian principles." I asked him how he could teach something so violent and still maintain Christian principles, but he wasn't able to give me a good answer. So after an hour of conversing with him, I knew he had already made up his mind and nothing I said was going to change his thinking.

The kids were often allowed to run around in church with their uniforms on. One day, the instructor went to the pastor (who apparently did not have a clue what is behind the martial arts) and asked him if he minded if the kids called him "master." The pastor had a problem with that and he responded, "There is only one master—Jesus!" But the instructor did it anyway. He even had an email address in which he called himself master so and so. That sounds like pride and rebellion to me. Those are the character traits that are inherent in those who participate in martial arts, so this story is not at all surprising.

There are numerous sports activities that can provide children physical fitness, as well as give them confidence, coordination, and teamwork mentality. They are fun and give young people an outlet for the seemingly unlimited energy they possess. (It would be great if we could bottle that energy and save it until later in life!) Many sports teach sport etiquette, character, and respect.

There are some sports that are more physically dangerous than others, but none have the spiritual ramifications that are found in all martial arts! Also, in the martial arts it is not just about physical fitness, friendly competition, etiquette, or respect. It is about pride and anger, and it is about winning, no matter the cost. No other sport takes one far beyond the physical aspect and into the unseen, spiritual realm like martial arts. It simply cannot be compared to other sports; I don't even call it a sport!

Success in the martial arts depends on many factors. It starts out as how to defend oneself, but almost immediately evolves into how to use offensive, very violent tactics. Out of necessity, one must learn how to use his newly-acquired skills to actually hurt the other person, or persons. This simply cannot be done with a passive attitude. *It takes aggressiveness and violent action, which are deeply embedded in the psychological and physical training methods in all martial arts.*

There are no exceptions—all have a violent developmental history. The intent has been, and will always be, to take the other person out! That requires training that develops kicking, punching, and other techniques that could seriously injure a person, or even kill them. Otherwise, why go through the martial arts training just for the exercise, when one can get exercise in a lot of other ways? In the martial arts, you will get the whole package, whether you want it or not. It is all built in.

By its very nature, involvement in the martial arts (of any kind) will plant seeds after its kind. As I stated in an earlier chapter, a seed (an acorn) from an oak tree will only produce an oak tree. One cannot change the DNA from its original design and purpose. It is both a natural and a spiritual law that everything will always produce "after its kind." A seed sends down roots before it produces a tree.

It is the thought and the intent that controls the actions one takes, so the inner person must be transformed in order to commit the outer physical acts. The seeds of violence are planted and cultivated until they become mature and useful for the intended purpose. The long-term effects will manifest in many different ways, such as pride, rebellion, anger/rage, aggressiveness, intimidation, cockiness, provoking, and a general feeling of invincibility.

I want to share an experience that happened some years ago, which changed my life forever. I was the head referee, which meant because of my rank and experience in the martial arts, I had control and I made the final decisions in this particular Karate tournament. There were around 200-250 people gathered in a school gymnasium for what was to be a friendly day of competition. There were about 80-90 competitors. Many of the competitors were young children six to twelve years old. It was the early stage of the competition that I want to focus on here.

We had arranged for the youngest children to compete first so they would not get bored or tired because it was going to be a long day. These cute kids were warming up by stretching and practicing their moves, much like they would in any sport, getting themselves ready for the big day of competition. For many, they were going to compete and test their skills for the very first time. They were both excited and nervous, each waiting for his or her turn to enter the ring to which they were assigned, to face all the unknowns.

Their club instructors and their parents seemed more confident and ready than the kids did. What struck me more than anything else was the fear I saw on some of their young faces. I could only imagine what was going on inside them, and I now know it took more than just their physical skills to drive them forward.

There are often many clubs (dojos) represented at these tournaments (just like in "The Karate Kid") with various styles, taught by a diverse number of coaches and training methods—good, bad, and ugly—some very ugly! Many of these Karate styles were better suited for competition than others. Some were not well equipped at all. Open tournaments often bring out the weird, the bizarre, and the wacky attitudes and behavior of students, which is a reflection of that which they picked up from their instructors. Oftentimes, there has been a transfer of attitude (and more) to the students and they often become clones of their instructor.

I personally never did like the idea of children competing in martial arts tournaments. I knew the psychological dangers as well as the very real possibility of physical injuries. But, because parents wanted their children trained and the economic possibilities presented cash flow, I pushed past the obstacles in my mind.

Also, I was very busy with adult groups all around the Midwest at the time, so I mostly had my more advanced students train the children. The phenomenon of children getting involved in the martial arts was spreading like wildfire back then, but even more so today. My concern was, and still is, the physical and spiritual wellbeing of especially vulnerable, innocent children. Except in a couple of rare instances, I never trained children personally.

Having said all that, here I was in the midst of this tournament, which I thought was going well, when suddenly, for the first time in all my years in the martial arts, my eyes and ears were opened. I saw and heard evil and violence all around me. I heard what was coming from the spectators, directed at the two young boys in the ring where I was the referee. It was as if everything around me went into slow motion as these two kids were trying to score points on each other. These students had been trained to compete with no outward show of emotion, especially fear, but as I looked at them, I saw terror on the face of one, and on the other facial distortions full of rage!

Thoughts were racing through my mind. It seemed almost surreal. I thought, *What is happening to me? Is this my imagination, or is it real? What am I seeing?—has it always been there? Is this normal?* I saw something peering out of the boys that was spiritual in nature, and I could not explain it at the time. I was a new Christian of about nine months and did not know about spiritual powers, even though I had some very spooky, dangerous ones operating through me at the time. (Since I have been set free, it is much easier to identify and explain what is happening.)

Here were these two kids (around nine or ten years old), one trying to overpower the other with this violent look, and the other doing all he could to protect himself, with a determination to simply be able to survive this match. (I believe all of this was in slow motion so that I could really see what was going on.) It was not just what I saw in the ring that startled me, it was also what was coming from the stands.

As I turned and looked around me and saw the angry, contorted faces and some vile gestures towards these two young boys, it went straight to my heart like an arrow. The spectators were chanting and screaming, "Kill him, kill him, take his head off, knock him down! Don't back down!" It was a slow-motion nightmare, and I had a sick feeling in the pit of my stomach that I had never felt before. I knew I had to put a stop to all the madness around me, as parents were telling their kids to kill each other.

I stepped into the ring between the two boys and stopped the match—to the utter amazement of this hostile crowd. I was not going to let this mad frenzy go on any longer! I stood silently between the two boys, who were looking intently at me, wondering what was going to happen next. The entire gymnasium became eerily silent as I stood there looking around at them for nearly five minutes (or at least it seemed that long). I never said a word as all eyes were on me. You could have heard a pin drop. The silence was deafening.

As I stood there, I pondered the words that were coming in slow motion into my mind and my heart. My spiritual eyes and ears were receiving revelation as to what was really behind what I was involved in, and what I was sensing was an overwhelming shame. I heard these words in my spirit: "Look at what you have created; do you want to continue in this violence and evil?" Those words and this gut-wrenching experience were about to change the course of my life.

Finally, I spoke and a hush fell over everyone in the gym—audience and competitors alike—as they looked at me with dumbfounded expressions. I asked them, "Is this what you want?" I said, "Listen to yourselves...telling your children to kill one another! You're wanting your children to injure one another; you're calling for blood! These are your children. Is this your desire? What are you thinking? Or are you?"

My words were sending shock waves to all in attendance, as I was led (not even knowing it at the time) by the Holy Spirit. The words I spoke went straight to the hearts of every person there, whether they wanted to hear it or not. I continued, "Is this what we have come to? Calling for blood?" I know now (but at the time I didn't realize) the impact my words were having and how they would not only change me, but others who were there that day.

I knew then that something had changed in me. I recognized that before my Christian experience and conversion, I was the leader (coach, sensei) who was just like them and that they had become just like I used to be. I was the one responsible for creating this monster and I didn't even know it! But after that eye-opening experience, I knew the God that I now believed in was convicting me and showing me this activity was not of Him!

It came about a few months later at another tournament (which I was not actively involved in, but one in which many of my students participated) that *it was time to give it up.* I addressed a stunned crowd who knew me well. *I demonstrated that for years I had wrapped this black belt around me and that it had become my confidence, my strength, my personality, my identity, and my life...but no longer would I embrace the martial arts. As* people listened in total silence, I told them I was now wrapping the gospel of love—Jesus Christ—around me and that He was all I needed and He was the one I would put my trust in.

Many of my students around the country (as well as instructors who knew me) were now very disappointed and some were even angry with me because they felt I had betrayed them, and the martial arts. The organizations that I had belonged to dissociated themselves from me and expunged from their records all former accolades, titles, and rankings I had achieved. Welcome to persecution for the gospel's sake! This was my first persecution experience, but it certainly would not be my last! I never condemned any of them for what they chose to remain in, but it was clear they knew where I stood.

The parents and competitors who attended the day I gave up the martial arts heard the words I spoke, and I believe some of them were changed for the better as a result. I would like to be able to tell you that this was the end of my involvement in the martial arts—unfortunately, it wasn't. (You will see what I mean when you read Chapter 7.)

In bringing this chapter to a conclusion, I want to leave you with this last bit of information. There are documented injuries that I received in my own body from years of repetitive movements, which did not show up until years later in my life. I am not alone. For many, there will be debilitating and permanent damage to the body, especially to the joints, hands, ankles, knees, hips, and spine because of the unnatural body movements which are repeated thousands of times. Many of the resulting injuries also come from physical contact with other people and from doing crazy feats such as breaking concrete blocks with one's bare hand or foot. What does that prove, other than stupidity?

These are the hooks:

The promoters of martial arts will tell you about *all the physical benefits, but never about the detrimental physical and spiritual ramifications.*

This is the bait:

It's great family fun! Learn self-defense! It will build your self-confidence, self-control, and mental discipline. It's a great sport! It will increase your self-awareness and self-knowledge! *(Notice how it's all about "self.")*

The typical advertisement:

- Master instructor 40 years
- Grand Master 8th, 9th, or 10th degree black belt
- Personal mastery through the martial arts
- We will take you to the top – unseal your potential!
- Mixed martial arts (as seen on TV)
- The ultimate fighting arts
- Combat martial arts
- Weapons training of all kinds
- Our students learn how to lead, how to win!
- Or how about this one?: Christian Karate Center

Some reasons not to enroll yourself or your children:

1. People are very impressionable, especially children. They are highly influenced by the razzle-dazzle, mystery, and fancy moves.

2. There is no way to extract violence from a violent act (or intent) such as smashing another person's face, or other such thing.

3. It is impossible to separate the natural aspect from the spiritual aspect. What happens in the spiritual (unseen) realm always affects the natural (visible) realm, and vice versa.

4. One becomes a planting field where seeds of pride, anger, violence, rebellion, deception, aggressiveness, and intimidation have a place to grow up and possibly be transferred to others (or others may be adversely affected by these things). Not everyone is a candidate for all these traits, but how does one know until it's too late?

5. Once people open themselves up to the forces that are connected in the spiritual realm, those unseen forces now have a "legal right" to operate in that person's life, whether they know it or not, or whether they want them or not. Once that door is opened, that person receives everything that is connected with it!

6. Things will pop up, influence, and possibly control areas of one's life because of the *occult nature* and operation that has been allowed access. In other words, it's quite possible you will see a behavior change and certain traits coming to the forefront that never existed in your child before his or her involvement in the martial arts. At some point in their training, they will probably have an urge to "test their newfound skills," and may just be looking for an opportunity to provoke a fight with their siblings or others.

Parents may have a difficult time explaining to their children why they should no longer be involved, but I would suggest that you seek wisdom as to the right approach in undoing any damage that has already been done. For those who profess to be Christians who have already allowed these influences to affect their children (and for those adults who have involved themselves in martial arts) an act of repentance and renunciation of their involvement is in order. If, by now, you are sensing that it is time for you to get out, there is a prayer (at the end of the book) that will close this doorway and remove the legal right.

CHAPTER 6

SECRETS BEHIND THE MARTIAL ARTS & YOGA REVEALED

THE PEOPLE IN WESTERN CULTURES, for the most part, are simply ignorant about the religious and spiritual realities that connect all forms of martial arts and yoga practices. (Or they have pretended or denied that this connection exists.) They will very often claim that they are not practicing an eastern religion, and that there is no spiritual connection. Back when I was training and instructing in the martial arts, I was often questioned by those wanting to get involved in martial arts as to the influence of the spiritual realm and the source of the power behind the practice of martial arts. Some were smart enough to have the insight that *you don't get something from nothing.*

At the time (because of my own ignorance) I would try to explain away the power source by demonstrating some basic techniques to try to convince them that there was nothing mystical, it was only physical, and no more than that. That is the same deception that I (and many other instructors and gurus) have used to try to convince the uninformed to accept. It wouldn't be until years later and a lot of heartache that I would fully understand the gut-wrenching feeling I had tried to ignore when I first became involved. It would take over thirty years to fully understand the truth and be set totally

> It is impossible to separate the spiritual aspect from the physical aspect!

free! I say once again for emphasis: It is impossible to separate the spiritual aspect from the physical aspect!

Let us examine the facts that reveal the truth. If a martial arts master or yoga guru is honest, he will tell you that one cannot separate the spiritual from the physical aspect in any of these arts, no matter how hard one attempts to do so. Those who claim they can are highly deceived (and desiring to deceive the western world), or they know very little about the historical "spiritual" root system and power source. Allow me to show how intricately they are integrated.

Do you remember that it was the indigenous people groups of India and China and other eastern cultures who over thousands of years ago were practicing various forms of shamanism, magic, and mysticism, etc., long before the fighting arts were introduced? They were the gullible, open-minded candidates who readily and freely accepted the various methods and practices of meditation introduced by Indian monks.

Remember that I said earlier that one of the most influential and important figures who contributed to their culture was Bodhidharma, who lived between the fifth and sixth century A.D. He introduced his brand of Hindu yoga meditation and fighting form that included physical fitness, mixed with all the other spiritual practices, which made for a very potent form of martial arts. Bodhidharma's Zen practice of Hindu yoga was, in essence, the "martial arts in motion." Through their Zen disciplines of mind, body, and spirit, one was supposedly able to achieve what is called "enlightenment" by the Hindus and Buddhists.

Today, this "so-called" enlightenment is known as a *spiritual experience*, which is a term used by all occult practitioners, i.e. those in New Age, Wicca, witchcraft, spiritualism, shamanism, and many other variations. Meditation is one of the methods those involved in the occult use for channeling. In essence, this is opening oneself up spiritually to the dark side, allowing evil spirits to move in, operate through, or speak through those who open themselves up to this spiritual realm.

I am not saying that all meditation is bad. As a Christian, God encourages us to meditate on His Word, His truth, and His promises, and be filled with His Spirit, so that we can partake of His divine nature and walk in His power and truth. Most importantly, He never tells us to "clear our minds," but rather focus (meditate) on His truth, and be transformed in our inner man by renewing our minds according to His Word. (See Romans 12:1-2)

I have studied under senseis (instructors) who didn't directly talk much about the mind or meditation, but on every occasion we were told to "clear your mind," before and after each training session. It is this discipline that allows what is called the "ki" or "ch'i" to flow through the practitioner. Why clear the mind? To allow unhindered access! All martial arts and yoga incorporate the practice of "open-mindedness" through meditation techniques.

This meditation, which is practiced by those in the martial arts, can be done from a sitting or kneeling position, but more often is practiced by focusing or concentrating on various techniques of kicking, punching, and striking, and simultaneously incorporating certain breathing techniques in order to capture the mysterious "ki." Aikido (which means the "way of harmony with ki") was developed in 1942 by martial arts innovator Morihei Ueshiba. His goal with this martial art was deeply religious.

The basic concept that is taught is that "ki" (the universal power or energy source) *could be tapped into on an individual level* by breathing in and partaking of that universal power. This is a fundamental concept taught in all forms of martial arts and yoga! (In yoga, it is taught that it can be awakened or aroused from within the person and they claim it is latent within every human being.) This claim, of course, is false!

Morihei's Aikido employed a series of flowing circular movements—in conjunction with locking, holding, moving, and tumbling techniques—to attempt to turn an opponent's force against himself. These techniques are showcased in the action movies of popular Hollywood star, Steven Seagal.

There are some Oriental masters who will tell you openly that Karate, Kung Fu, Aikido, Judo, etc., is Zen, that it depends on Zen practices in order to be effective, and that Zen is required by all who practice martial arts, without exception. (However, most will not tell you that.) Zen is a philosophy and practice of Buddhism. The purported aim of Zen is to awaken the student to his true self and bring about a high degree of self-knowledge, through inward meditation.

It is also their goal to tap into the "so-called" latent power, or energy that they claim lies dormant in all people. They also believe that through meditation one can find peace of mind through this enlightened awakening, which is supposedly achieved through exercises, concentration, and empty-mindedness. This, in turn, becomes a spiritual experience definitely connected to Hinduism or Buddhism.

All martial arts and yoga practitioners, in some degree or another, experience by virtue of their involvement, aspects of the spiritual realm. All masters in Zen Buddhism know that these arts are an extension of their religious practices and involve the spiritual emphasis that they believe harmonizes the mind and body with the "so-called" universal energy. So how can western societies, steeped in western culture, think they can separate the two philosophies?

Students are trained in practice that to think first and act second is "too time consuming." "If one thinks about what he is going to do, it may be too late to react," they are told. "Allow the spirit in you to react," they say. (I never questioned what kind of spirit at the time!) It must be total instinct, allowing the body to mindlessly flow. In other words, when one empties the mind, it becomes an empty container, waiting for something to occupy it, but what?

In the cult movie "Star Wars" series, we hear the voice of Obi-Wan Kenobi, a Jedi master, speak to his apprentice, "Luke, clear your mind, let the force flow through you; let the force do its work; the force be with you!" This is presented as both sides of the "so-called" Jedi – the dark and light side. (Jedi sounds like the concept of yin and yang, doesn't it?)

Again, it is this same concept that one finds in the martial arts. As Selwyn Stevens says, many times students are "taught that the Shaolin monk walked the 'right path' while those in opposition followed the 'wrong path.' Thus there in their history was waged a continual war between the 'black' yogis and the 'white' yogis. The object or goal of the martial artist is to achieve perfect balance, or harmony of the yin and yang. [They believe that] only then is he able to control the life force (ch'i) with which he believes he can achieve his objectives in overcoming an opponent."[1]

Although practitioners, especially in the West, tend to disregard much of the Zen philosophy and practices in their training, some impact of that philosophy is transferred to every student of these arts—no exceptions! This is because meditation and yoga-like breathing exercises, and the clearing of one's mind, whether for thirty seconds or for two hours, before or after every practice session, will have an impact on every practitioner.

The key in all occult practices is the blank mind, i.e. empty mind, in order to let outside forces in, to operate through a person. Without this passive state of empty mindedness, the occult power has no access point and is not able to enter and give that person supernatural ability. Consequently, all martial arts moves, whether defending or attacking, have inherent spiritual implications.

When one looks at the many varied movements in some of these arts, one can see the unnatural hand and foot positions, along with unnatural facial contortions. Not to mention the weird noises that I talked about in a previous chapter! Also, they often imitate positions and movements of insects, birds, and animals such as tigers and monkeys. How bizarre! All of these things should be a clue!

All systems of martial arts, whether hard style or soft style, have the same DNA. Every move has a name and a meaning. Nearly every position and every breathing exercise is designed to connect to the power source. Only a small percentage (around ten percent) of the superhuman feats are accomplished from a purely physical standpoint. The other ninety-percent of their ability is because of the spiritual forces operating through them.

So in order to connect to the flow (*which has never been something that is latent within*) one must draw it in from outside of one's natural body. The supernatural power inherent in the martial arts has never been attained from physical training alone, nor has it ever come from some force that is latent within, but it is always from external forces. The instructors all say, "It takes body, mind, and spirit coordination." I prefer to call it cooperation—giving permission and allowing an outside force access to use one's body.

Through the process of emptying the mind, it becomes a container, a channel or doorway, just waiting for something to enter or fill it. As a student, I remember well the instructions I received thousands of times from my instructors, "Vito-san, clear your mind; let the spirit flow; you need more spirit." I didn't understand that what he was prodding me to do was to have a supernatural experience. I thought he was telling me to have more enthusiasm, like excitement at a football game, like school spirit.

That is not what he wanted me to have. He wanted and encouraged me to receive not only psychic ability, but also supernatural power to react or perform some function. That would require a takeover of my body—an incorporation of the spiritual with the physical. Without knowing, I was opening my mind and my body up to the occult spirit realm. (I now know the extreme danger of doing that.)

That same spiritual energy or power that accompanies all martial arts feats can also be transferred to the student by the simple touch of the instructor or other students. What is often not talked about or exposed is the fact that this transference takes place. The practice of "laying on of hands" is as old as mankind and is effective, whether for good or evil, a blessing or a curse. In Christian and Jewish traditions, they understand the benefit of laying on of hands to impart a blessing. What they are doing by faith is a spiritual concept that we are told to do in order to release the power of God's blessings.

In the martial arts (and related arts) there is also a spiritual transfer, usually working through the instructor who himself has been affected by a spiritual force working through someone else—his own instructor.

So what I mean by transfer from them was not a good spiritual power, but an evil entity that has taken up residence in them, using them as their vessel to flow through—their "so-called" energy flow.

It was on occasions where my instructors corrected my stance or position when performing training techniques that I felt this touch and a jolt or transfer of power that went inside my body. Afterward, I felt different and moved differently, with more intensity and focus. Something he had transferred to me now had a measure of control over my body and my mind, whether I wanted it or not.

Martial arts instruction requires, at times, the laying on of hands or touching another person in a way that one would not normally touch another person. One example would be a male instructor who needs to correct the incorrect posture or stance of a female student and would need to touch the hips, the legs, the neck, or other parts of the body in order to show her what was done incorrectly.

Close body-to-body contact very often takes place between opposite sex partners who are practicing various moves, especially self-defense techniques. Full body contact is sometimes required and necessary. It is impossible to prevent personal parts of the bodies from touching each other. Impure thoughts can easily result because of the extremely close physical contact. Pretty soon, you have people committing adultery, fornication, or fantasizing about another student, whether married or not. You might be saying, "No way!" But it happens. Over the years, I have talked to instructors and students alike who told me that is exactly what happened to them!

The instructor has, in essence, control over those who submit to his authority. He is the master, the guru of your life, so you believe whatever he tells you and obey his every command in unquestioning obedience. To those who submit in that way, he becomes the master to be worshipped and idolized as a god figure. I have a real problem when people want to be known and spoken of as a master. Bowing to a master is an act of submission, which opens one up automatically to the same spirit that operates in the master. There can be and is a transference of knowledge and/or power, but it is definitely from the satanic realm.

There is a master (Satan himself) over the secretive occult realm who is given authority to rule in peoples' lives when they choose to bow down to him or submit to his influence. At that point, they choose to come under his authority. In the Bible (Second Corinthians 4:4 KJV) Satan is called the "god of this world." Why is he called the "god of this world?" Because in the Garden of Eden, when Adam chose to listen to Eve (who had listened to the serpent—the devil), and Adam consequently chose to disobey God, Adam and Eve lost the authority that God had given them to rule and have dominion on this earth.

This principle of authority having been transferred is evident where we see Satan tempting Jesus. Luke 4:6-7 says, "And the devil said to Him, 'All this authority I will give You, and their glory; for this has been delivered to me, and I give it to whomever I wish. Therefore, if You will worship before me, all will be Yours.'" Notice that Jesus did not refute the fact that the devil had received this authority and power. Jesus simply chose not to come under the devil's influence, authority, or power. Instead, He quoted the written Word of God, by saying in Verse 8, "Get behind Me, Satan! For it is written, 'You shall worship the Lord your God, and Him only you shall serve.'"

Again, I repeat for emphasis, it was the meditation behind yoga-type practices, which was the source and method used to gain self-awareness and self-knowledge (so-called enlightenment) and was what originally gave birth to the martial arts. Consequently, it is fair to say that both have much in common and are connected by the spiritual energy forces known as "ki" or "ch'i" or prana. Through various methods of meditation, aligning the body through the different positions, along with required "special" breathing exercises, one opens the channel for the spirit power (or so-called energy) to operate in and through oneself.

All martial arts incorporate some form of meditation through "breathing exercises," by which practitioners acquire the mysterious power called "ki." The mysterious power is not a mystery at all. It has a source of origination. It comes from a place, a realm, and is *not some form of benign energy*, floating around the cosmos, waiting to be tapped into by human beings, as many believe. Neither is it an energy force that is found latent within all human beings, waiting to be drawn out. If it were just a benign energy force, it would be harmless, innocent, and non-threatening. But, in fact, it is *malignant!* Webster's definition of "malignant" which applies here is this: "Evil in nature, influence, or effect; injurious; aggressively malicious."[2] *It is a malignant force that has been at war with mankind for thousands of years.*

Once that person has that power, it must be released in order to accomplish its purpose. In martial arts, "ki" or "ch'i" is power that is transferred to a point of contact with explosive force to an intended target, either imagined or real. Whether it is breaking boards, or blocks, or striking a person, there is a transfer of that energy by touch (or contact).

Once again, without the use of the "ki" or "ch'i" force, it would be no different than boxing or other contact sports. There would be no supernatural energy force empowering that person, only physical power. In the martial arts, it is much more than physical power alone, and every student is subject to the transference of this supernatural power simply by virtue of their choice to become involved.

Notes

1. Selwyn Stevens, *Insights Into Martial Arts,* (Wellington, New Zealand: Jubilee Resources, 2005) p. 16
2. Merriam *Webster's Collegiate Dictionary,* Tenth Edition (Springfield, MA: Merriam-Webster, Inc., 1997).

CHAPTER 7

OUT OF DARKNESS INTO THE LIGHT – MY NEW IDENTITY

WHEN I WAS GROWING UP, I was small in stature due to a childhood illness that nearly took my life at the age of two. Even when I was in my teens, I was still shorter than average and, as a result, I was bullied by older, bigger guys. Even two of my older brothers used to take advantage of me, by bossing and pushing me around. One day, after putting up with this for years, *I vowed that I would not be told what to do or pushed around anymore by anyone!* So, as a result, I decided the only way to come out on top was to become more aggressive. I grew up in a fairly rough neighborhood and I just knew I had to stand up for myself or be run over by some bully.

God had a good plan for my life, but the devil tried to stop God's plan. I believe that my "near-death" experience at two years old was an attempt by the enemy to snuff me out. For whatever reason, he didn't want my destiny to come to pass and although he didn't have the full knowledge of what that destiny held, he certainly did not want it to be fulfilled.

I had a gifting that was not yet fully developed when I was growing up, which was a part of my life for as long as I can remember. I believe all children have an extra sensitivity to what is going on around them, but I had discernment (some may call it intuition or something else) and I could see things before they happened. I could also discern what kind of spirit was operating in people.

At an early age, I hungered for spiritual things, but I could never seem to find what I was looking for. I remember a cold, clear December night when I was about 15 or 16. I was reminiscing about what I had experienced thus far in my life and I wondered about my future. I saw myself where I was, and I sensed where I was headed, and somehow I knew it wasn't good.

I looked up into the clear, starlit sky and spoke aloud, "Is there a God? Why am I here? What is my purpose? Why did you spare my life? If you are real, what do you want me to do?" I didn't hear any answer, and at the time, I decided that God either did not exist or did not care. I remember saying aloud, "Well, God, I guess you just don't care!" Did God hear me? Absolutely! Did the devil also hear me? Yes.

I knew the difference between right and wrong and although I was raised as a Roman Catholic, I did not have a strong spiritual understanding, as I had not yet had a real personal encounter with God. The world was taking precedence in my life because of my lack of spiritual understanding. I became an easy target for the enemy. Because I had decided that God did not care, I began to move further and further away from God and into darkness. I knew God had given me gifts, but I lacked direction and godly counsel. It was the dark side that would begin to win and take charge of my life at that point.

Later, in 1959, at the age of 19, I enlisted in the Marine Corps. I was about to be toughened even more as I endured rigorous training in boot camp where I was taught to be a "lean, mean, killing machine." I learned not only how to use weapons, but also hand-to-hand techniques as well. This was actually a form of martial arts, techniques derived from Judo and Jujitsu. It came naturally for me, because I had already learned on the mean streets of North St. Louis that backing down or showing fear was not an option. Neither was losing. I was determined to come out on top.

The Marine Corps had taught me discipline. That training was a precursor for what was to become thirty more years of involvement in the martial arts. Shortly after I finished my tour of duty, I heard about a Judo club near Washington University in my hometown—St. Louis. It was October of 1961. I went there, but didn't stay long because the instructor taught Judo and I was more interested in learning Karate. A few months later, my job transferred me to Chicago, and it was there I began to search in earnest for a qualified Karate instructor.

One day while driving to work, I saw one of those red and white Karate signs with the rising sun (which represents the Japanese flag) on the second floor of a commercial building. A few weeks later, I dropped in to see what was going on. Upon entering, I had to climb a long set of stairs, which in the months to come would be climbed numerous times. Many times I would be so sore from the previous day's training, I could hardly make it to the top. Even though I was not yet a Christian, the first time I climbed those stairs and stepped into that dojo, *I knew in my spirit something was not right!*

I was met by a tall Japanese man in a white robe, wearing a black belt, who spoke very little English. I immediately observed several things.

- I had never seen a Japanese man who was that tall. He was about five feet, ten inches tall and weighed about 175 pounds.

- He was very well conditioned, physically.

- He was clean and polite.

- He exuded great confidence and he had an "aura" around him that was intimidating.

Using hand gestures and broken English, he asked me what I wanted and why I wanted to study Karate. I knew he was screening me, so I could not tell him the full reason why I was interested, which (at the time) was to become knowledgeable and physically equipped to "kick butt with style." Little did I know at that time, I would get much more than I bargained for. So, I told him I wanted to study for the arts' sake. What a joke!

His name was Shojiro Sugiyama, and when he looked at me I could almost see the smirk behind his smile. He knew I wasn't completely honest and he had a pretty good idea what my real intentions were, but he accepted me as a good potential candidate. The very next day the training began.

Was I in for a surprise! I walked in and started for the dressing room when I was suddenly stopped in my tracks by a very authoritative voice that shouted, "Stop!" My heart nearly stopped at the sound of his voice. I was astonished by the harsh look on his face and his hands on his hips. The class was about to start, which consisted of about six to eight other beginners. They, too, were startled by his sudden outburst. I stood perfectly still—not knowing what was going to happen next.

I thought the day I stepped off the bus at Parris Island, South Carolina at the Marine Corps depot was a wakeup call of sorts, but this was bone chilling to say the least. I was glad I had control of my bladder or there would have been a mess. My heart was pounding and I didn't know exactly what to say, so I said something really stupid like, "What?" I might as well have walked over to him and slapped him on the shoulder and said, "What's up, old buddy?" Needless to say, my "What?" was almost as bad. I was quickly informed of proper Japanese etiquette and manners.

I was ignorant about other cultures, so I thought I could just act myself and just be "a good ole boy," but that didn't go over well in a Japanese-run dojo. They require complete respect, not only to the instructor, who is called a sensei (master), but also toward everyone present. Mr. Sugiyama pointed to my shoes and in broken English said something to this effect: "Take them off before entering the practice area and acknowledge to everyone present that you are here by bowing and saying 'oos'." I thought, *Are they blind? They can see me.*

The Japanese word "oos" can be used in several different ways. It can be used as a greeting of arrival or departure, it can signify that you are ready, or that you understand the command just given. In the months ahead, the commands would be barked out so loud and so clear that it made the commands and instructors in the Marine Corps seem like child's play.

The training was like nothing I had ever experienced. My body ached like never before. Fatigue was the order of the day and watching this man move with intensity and determination shook me to the core. I thought on many occasions that I might be in something deeper than what I originally thought or intended. This was brutal training and it only got more intense as the weeks went by. The repetitions wore on my body and my mind. I thought, *How can a human being endure this kind of punishment? And I'm paying for this?*

But somehow those who would succeed would endure and the numbers were very few indeed. I learned to keep my mouth shut, saying as little as possible, and I tried to stay in the background so I wouldn't be noticed. But it didn't work; it seemed his eyes were always on me, no matter where I was. It seemed he had eyes in the back of his head. That was kind of spooky.

I bought my first gi (Karate uniform) which was a training outfit that consisted of a two-piece white top and bottom with a white belt, which I proudly wore. Now I was like everyone else and I felt I now fit in with the rest of the class. The rigorous training kept getting tougher, not easier, as I had previously thought it would. My cigarette smoking didn't help matters either, as I was often struggling to breathe. Mr. Sugiyama knew this and on many occasions rebuked me for smoking, so I quickly learned not to carry my cigarettes or my lighter in my pocket when I entered the gym.

I wouldn't hear the last of it; in fact, I always paid the price. Not only did the smoking affect my breathing, but he made me do extra reps and other training to try to break me of smoking. He would say, "You stink of smoke!" His harassment did not work. It was years later that God would sovereignly deliver me of nicotine addiction, but at that time, I had not met the Lord yet, so I was pretty much "on my own." The constant harassment of my instructor just made me angry and more determined than ever to succeed.

My training continued and I never paid attention or even really noticed that I was progressing at a very fast pace. I was excelling in my abilities much faster than most people do and it was certainly noticed by everyone except me. I only wanted to train and be the best I could be. The first nine months of my training period proved rather interesting. I took rank exams for various belts and I was progressing so fast that I even skipped belts on the way up. The Japanese belt system for the U.S. students went from white to yellow to blue to green, then two degrees of purple, three degrees of brown, and then first-degree black belt.

I went from white to green to purple, then brown in nine months. This was unheard of and quite a feat for anyone! The best was yet to come. I had been a brown belt for less than three months when Grand Master Masatoshi Nakayama (a 9th degree black belt) visited the Chicago dojo where I was training. They decided to hold a special rank exam for some other brown belts who were trying to make their black belts. I had just come up to watch the proceedings, when I was summoned and told to put my uniform on (which I kept there in a locker). There I was—a fresh, brand new, still "wet behind the ears" brown belt of only a few weeks, being told to go through training techniques that I had learned along with the others who were being tested.

I had no idea why I was asked to be on the floor with them, but I was not going to refuse to do what my instructor asked of me, especially in front of this board of black belts. I had learned not to argue early on when four top Japanese champions, all 5th degree black belts, came to Chicago prior to that day. I had just earned the highest rank of purple belt and sparred with these guys. What a joke! I thought, *They could kill me at any time.* They were the scariest people on the face of the earth—mean and violent!

Here I was standing before the master of Shotokan Karate, Mr. Nakayama, and seated to his right and left were a board of several other high-ranking Japanese black belts. Even though I wondered why I was out there with the others, I wasn't going to be outdone and not do my best, no matter what their reason was for having me perform before the board. When all was finished, which took about 25 minutes, I went back and changed into street clothes, glad that I was done and now able to watch the rest of the students go through their exams.

When I came back out of the dressing room, I was called up front and, much to my surprise, presented a black belt by Mr. Nakayama. I was literally shocked and so was everyone else except the board of examiners. Although I did not meet the criteria for the required length of time (which was usually around two years before one could take a shodan test for black belt) they made an extraordinary exception. They awarded me and promoted me to the rank of black belt. I was a candidate they felt they could use!

At that time, I was the only non-Japanese person in the world to attain a black belt in less than a year. I couldn't believe it, but I wasn't going to turn it down. I had never tried to achieve degrees. At the time, that was not my interest. I only wanted to excel in my ability in the martial arts, not attain different color belts. The belt is only as good as the person's ability anyway and I knew from my own experience that ability spoke louder than the color of one's belt, as I often out-performed those of higher rank, both before and after that particular day.

Well, the training continued at an even more accelerated pace after that, for the higher one went up the ladder of rank, the more advanced the training became. The challenge not only came from the difficulty from the physical standpoint, but from the mental as well. This was a new dimension and the mental challenges became so difficult that again I wanted to quit. I often wanted to pack it all in and say, "Enough is enough."

At times, I would even stop training for a couple of weeks, only to find myself drawn back again and again. I was addicted. I was hooked. It wasn't until years later, that I would understand what kept drawing me back. (I now know it was a soul tie to the "occult spirit behind the martial arts.") The longer I trained, the more I was changed. Karate had become my identity!

Karate had become my identity!

Something was happening and, at the time, I liked the changes. I experienced a high (a release of endorphins) much like runners and other athletes often experience. It was like a high all the time, but there was more—much more. I was not only becoming an expert and more aggressive, I was also demonstrating the ability to teach others and soon found myself assisting my instructor.

Within a year, I was teaching at one of his satellite dojos. The coaching position required me to become more proficient, so between coaching and training, my three-day week sessions became six to seven days a week. The more I trained, the more aggressive I became, and on many occasions, I injured my partners to the point that they did not want to work out with me. I didn't control my punch and kicking techniques enough, and I let whoever was in front of me know it. I was a no-nonsense person and I expected no less from the people I trained or worked out with. However, this *aggressiveness without control* was a lot worse than I realized at the time.

It wasn't until I had a revelation, after becoming a Christian in 1971, that I realized I had become like my instructor—aggressive, even violent at times. I had received what he had passed on to me. I believe that my martial arts training and my military training combined did help me control any really violent behavior, or I would have found myself in real trouble. I learned to discipline and channel my emotions and pent-up aggressiveness in a more positive direction. After I became a Christian, I realized this pent-up junk inside me was not Christlike, nor was I growing or moving forward in my Christian faith. Something was wrong. A force that I could not explain had attached itself to me and was controlling me.

My martial arts training would be tested on many fronts. When I began competing outside of the training dojos, I found that in competition my aggressiveness was out of control. My personality was one that most people liked and I easily associated with many people on a friendly social basis, but when it was time to put on my uniform and belt and step into the competition arena, I changed like a chameleon. I changed from day to night in attitude and no one was going to deprive me from dominating, winning, and beating my opponent. I simply went in to win—period!

In competition, we were not allowed to wear protective gear except a mouthpiece and groin protector. I wore neither, not even in normal practice times in the dojo! That is probably what made me move faster and smarter, and propelled me to always attack my opponent with such aggressiveness that they rarely stood a chance, unless they got real lucky and got one by me. On occasion they did. I competed later on in years with some very good competitors from Japan, California, Philadelphia, and New York when I started competing in national competitions.

We could wear shin and arm pads while training in the dojo to protect injured areas. Pads and protective equipment would hinder one's perfection of blocking and striking techniques. If they were not properly executed, one would pay the price. I never much liked equipment on my body. I felt it only slowed me down, or would make me more daring than I should be. I also felt it would cause me to depend on pads instead of proper execution of offensive and defensive techniques.

I immensely enjoyed a good match back then. It's not like today, where pads are worn for protection all over the body, which is good in a sense because of all the injuries people incur. In some styles of martial arts, they have nearly every part of their body padded up with some kind of foam product and plastic headgear, and they are allowed to try to bang up one another any way they want. In that case, they certainly don't focus on technique.

Some throwing, grabbing, and/or knocking-down techniques, in truth, are quite difficult with all the padding. In today's mixed martial arts, they only wear a mouthpiece and some hand protection, but in reality, they are trying to destroy one another any way they can. The long-term effects of this are going to be disastrous for those involved.

Whether in hard-style or soft-style martial arts, what it takes to excel in this activity opens one up to aggressive, even violent behavior. I do not believe you can train a person to be aggressive and violent, yet kind and compassionate at the same time. As a Christian, aggressiveness and violence is the diametric opposite of the fruit of the Holy Spirit in one's life.

In martial arts, one is supposedly taught to have self-control. It sounds good in theory, but experientially it can be a different story. I was taught to do all things "with control," stopping short by a quarter or a half-inch from the target, but that did not always happen. Especially with kicking techniques, if they were delivered too hard on the opponent's body, it often found the target with a "thump." If it was contact to the face, one stood a good chance of disqualification. I was often disqualified and lost tournaments because I just wanted to put the fear of me in them. After all, the ultimate goal of all martial arts is to learn how to maim and even kill one's opponent.

Over the years, I have trained thousands of students, both in private dojos and at several universities. I could pick out which ones (after only a few months' training) who had a propensity for violence and indeed they did develop into very aggressive students. They were on their way to becoming as I was, and how my instructor was, and how his instructor was. Every seed that is sown produces after its kind. We were producing like kind—people who could explode at the drop of a hat.

Most instructors don't know what is going on with most of their students outside of the dojo. But I found out, over time, what some of my students were involved in. Some were selling and using drugs; others tested their newfound skills on unsuspecting people; some picked fights; others were involved in white or black supremacist organizations, and so forth.

The words on the back of the membership cards stated that we were to endeavor to be honest, kind, sincere, have good character, and maintain high moral standards and integrity. It sounded good on paper, but for the most part, it wasn't worth the paper it was written on. I have seen very few that have trained for any length of time who maintained these moral principles. In fact, as confidence increased in their training and skills, so did immorality.

How could you be kind and honest to your opponent in competition when your sole intent was to try to take the other person's head off (theoretically, of course) with a punch or a kick? In theory, you are supposed to be of good character by agreeing not to harm or injure the other person—by using control, stopping just short of hurting him or her. Experientially, however, it didn't work that way, as many were injured, but usually not too seriously.

I remember one incident in New Orleans when I was in national competition. During the match, my competitor intentionally kicked at my fingers on my left hand and broke my ring finger. They stopped the match; I taped my two fingers together and went back into the ring to finish the match. I felt the rage and anger rise up in me and I just wanted to retaliate. I turned and kicked him in the side with such force I lifted him off his feet and he was propelled out of the ring. The sound of the crushing blow could be heard all over the gymnasium. I knew instinctively that I had inflicted a lot of damage to his body, possibly breaking his ribs. He refused to come back into the ring with me and I was declared the winner of the match, and went on to win the national title.

This was after I had become a Christian, so I was immediately convicted for the damage I had done. I repented and went to look for him to apologize and ask for his forgiveness. I was not able to locate him because he was probably on his way to the hospital. As I look back on those times, I realize that violence had reared its ugly head once again, even though I was a professing Christian. There's something wrong with that picture.

In today's mixed martial arts "full-contact" tournaments, cage fighting, etc., there is little to no control being used. Because the fighting and violence have escalated and people are looking for more blood and gore, I can only imagine the short term and long term injuries that will result—and possibly even death. In my training, if there would have been "full contact," many would have been permanently injured or killed. I saw associates around the country who were barely hit in strategic places by some of these well-trained experts and were laid up for months from the effects of injuries—broken jaws, arms, etc.

Gichin Funakoshi (who is called the father of modern-day Karate) coined the following phrase that we were all supposed to be guided by: "The purpose of martial arts competition is not in winning or losing, but the perfection of the character of its participants." Sounds good, but in reality it did not work that way.

Students take on the personality of their instructors and fellow students. Put them in an environment that stresses winning as the reason for their competition and all bets are off for good character development, at least in the martial arts. They will develop character all right, but what kind? One cannot see the roots growing from a seed under the surface below the ground; one can only see what is above the ground. The deep-rooted seeds of aggressiveness, anger, and violence may not be detected until years later and by that time, it may be too late—unless they are delivered, by the grace of God.

I have read what all the so-called experts have said, that there is nothing wrong with the martial arts, and that as a Christian, one can study the deep things of God and then go into the gym and learn how to dismantle the person God says to love. This philosophy is skewed and deceptive. Either you are going to be aggressive and violent and ready, if necessary, to smash someone's brain in, or not. So what's the purpose? Many say, "It's about self-defense."

There was a time I, too, believed that self-defense was a good tool for people to be trained in. I know that the military, police departments, and other organizations that are set up for the protection of people are required to train their people using skills developed in the martial arts. The training is limited, however; it is not the same as training in a dojo for any length of time. Also, the Special Forces, Navy Seals, Army Rangers, and others are well trained, but not in the same way as people in the dojo. They don't use meditation, bowing, etc. They simply train them in certain techniques that might be required in combat, or to preserve one's life under various conditions of war.

My instructors were very good—no, they were the best sent by Japan to the states. They were modern-day gladiators and although they were polite and courteous on the outside, on the inside they were the most aggressive and violent men I ever knew. Oftentimes, they exuded an intimidating power that was supernatural and struck awe and fear in the hearts of all who came near them. They carried the Bushido "warrior" spirit of violence and intimidation. Most also exuded much pride. This kind of spirit is in all forms of martial arts, whether it is Karate, Judo, Aikido, Tae Kwon Do, or Kung Fu, etc.

I have seen mild-mannered students change in front of my very eyes into aggressive, angry individuals because they were driven to the point of mental and physical exhaustion. Because they were physically broken down and in a weakened state, they would ask and invoke unseen forces to give them strength and power. They would say something like this: "Whatever this power and strength is that others have, I want it, no matter what it is."

At that point, they gave no thought as to what the source of that power might be. They received strong power, but it was evil and it altered their lives forever. An open door like that brought in all kinds of evil into their soul (their heart), which began to be acted out in their everyday lives. Sometimes, I wonder what happened to them over the years and I am impressed to pray for them that God would deliver them from this evil, even as He has delivered me.

Pride and ego go hand-in-hand in many martial arts practitioners. Speaking of pride and ego, mine was right at the top of the list. Back then, I was even prideful about the quality of the students I was producing. It has literally taken years for all the layers of junk that I picked up through my involvement in the martial arts to be removed from my life. But the most significant deliverance that occurred was when I got delivered from the violence I had picked up—the Bushido spirit. This happened a couple of years after I became a Christian. In fact, it was a day I will never forget. But, first, allow me to backtrack a bit.

In 1971, some of my college Karate students were in a small huddle after class, discussing a best-seller book by Hal Lindsey, *The Late Great Planet Earth*. This caught my attention and I asked them about the book. A few days later I went out and bought the book for myself. That same evening, I settled in my blue leather recliner to read the book. As I read,

I began to have a lot of questions. Was there really a God? Did He care for me?

At one point I said, "God, are you real? If so, how can I know for sure that I will not go to hell?" My question was quickly answered—as clear as a bell. I heard a voice in my spirit say, "If you really want to know, believe in My son, Jesus Christ." Then I responded, "What must I do?" I heard Him answer, "Son, repent, ask me for forgiveness, accept Jesus into your heart, and your life will turn around." I thought, *What have I got to lose? I have everything to gain.* Immediately I did as He said, and there was a cleansing—a refreshing that seemed to wash over me, and a peace that settled in on me.

Because my experience was not in a church, and because of my background and my ignorance of spiritual things (up to that point), I thought for a week or so that I must have had a great enlightenment, such as many of the masters had been telling me I needed. It was an enlightenment—but not the kind they were referring to! Somehow I knew in my heart this was different. My students, as well as others, sensed something had happened to me because all I wanted to do was talk about the things of God. I wanted to share my experience, but not everyone wanted to hear it. That didn't matter to me though. It didn't dampen my enthusiasm a bit, as I began to share with everyone I came in contact with, whether in a dojo or a grocery store! All I wanted to do was share the Good News.

About a year later, I knew the Lord was saying, "Give it up. I want you out of it." So, I walked away from the martial arts. (If you remember, I shared about the day I made that decision in the "Kids in Karate" chapter.) After the Lord impressed on me to give up the martial arts, it soon became apparent to me that I needed deliverance, especially from the strong spirit of violence.

Although I loved the Lord, I knew there were some things that troubled me about my past. I went to the pastor and he referred me to some people in the church. I told them I needed help. (Many Christians believe that once a person repents and says the "sinner's prayer," he or she is automatically completely free of any spiritual strongholds, but I knew that wasn't the case.)

That same day, a group of six of them agreed to pray with me at the church so that I could be free from any and all strongholds. These six people barely knew what to do. They had a teaspoon of knowledge when it would take a gallon to set me free. That in itself was dangerous, because the whole time they were trying to cast this evil spirit out, it was telling me it was going to kill me by running my head into the concrete block wall of the room we were in.

Then the evil spirit screamed aloud (through me) and said, "My name is Violence and I'm going to get you all!" I was terrified and they were, too. I said to them, "Don't let me go or it will kill me." So they, in their physical strength (a combined weight of roughly 1000 pounds) tried to hold me down. Unbelievably, the strength of that demon brought them all off the floor as if they were rag dolls.

As I look back on it now, I see how we all could have been injured, or worse, if not for the grace of God—a good reason not to go into the ministry of deliverance if you don't have proper training and know your authority! One of them had the good sense to use the name of Jesus. She quietly said "Jesus, Jesus, Jesus." The demon did leave, I was set free, and no one was hurt.

Here I was an enthusiastic zealot for God, and yet I had this other force still operating in me. Many would ask, "How can that be?" The truth is, there are numerous Christians out there who also need to be free from many different strongholds! Yet, because of a fallacy—widespread belief that Christians cannot be affected by demonic powers—many are still in bondage. I believe it is high time for that mindset to change so that the people of God can be totally set free.

Ironically, about two years after I gave up the martial arts, in obedience to the prompting of the Lord, a leading elder from the church I was now a part of came to me and asked me to start up a class in the church on self-defense. I balked at first because I didn't think that this violent sport belonged in the church. But, under the guise of self-defense, it sounded like a good thing that might benefit people, and after all, he was a leader in the church! (By the way, he was fascinated with the martial arts.) Because I was still a baby Christian, I just assumed that because he was a leader in the church, as well as a college professor, it must be okay—even though that still, small voice inside me was saying, "Don't do it!"

Unfortunately, I ignored that voice and I got back into it. I bought the lie that maybe God had said I had been out of it long enough and now I could go back into it, apply Christian principles in teaching it, and everyone could benefit from my expertise and knowledge. After all, we were teaching people how to protect themselves against violence. What could be wrong with that? It was also going to be used as an evangelistic tool, whereby we were hoping people would participate, and through that participation, we could minister the gospel to them somewhat indirectly. After all, we always had prayer before and after each session, as well as a short Bible study at the end.

Over a short time, however, it wasn't enough just to teach a few basic self-defense techniques. It escalated into full-blown Karate training for those who wanted more. Of course, I did it without the Japanese rituals and harshness that I had been trained under. It was now "Christian martial arts," or so I thought. Once again, I was deceived because I had allowed the enemy to twist my thinking.

When I was back in the ring, I was not in there for fun, or to show the love of God. I was not there to play "patty cake" with my opponent. My training kicked in again, and I was there to take my opponent out—to win at all costs (in love, of course). *In retrospect, I don't know how I thought I could teach a very violent activity in a non-violent way.* The problem is, at some point early on, that training crosses the line from self-defense to offense. Here I was once again, teaching students how to do great bodily harm to another human being.

I began to see the same things with the people I was training in church that I had seen in the secular arena—pride (superiority), violence, adultery, fornication, drugs, and the like. I didn't make the connection back then that it was because of the evil demonic influence behind the martial arts, that this had now opened a huge door into the church that had allowed the enemy access to people's lives. I continued in my own deception, thinking I could minister the truth to these people. Was I ever wrong!

The church thought it was a great outreach at first because people from the outside I had had connections with before began to come to these classes. However, most of these people never attended any of our regular church services, so it really didn't serve the purpose of being the evangelistic outreach it was envisioned to be. They only wanted to train under me.

This once vibrant, fast-growing church began to decline. The elder who had suggested I bring martial arts into the church eventually fell into adultery and thievery. Turmoil and division came into the church. The leaders were busy "putting out fires" here and there because many things began to go awry and they didn't know why. Was it all because of the martial arts? Probably not, but I do know it was a major contributor to the demise I began to see.

When I was born again, I knew I was called to be an evangelist. I had begun to do evangelistic outreaches on college campuses, in malls, in parks, and in prisons. I even put together and developed a martial arts demonstration team, using my past experience. I demonstrated various martial arts techniques, breaking boards and concrete blocks to get the "oohs" and the "aahs," which then set the stage to share the gospel.

Having a martial arts background was a drawing card that brought many in to see these exhibitions that would have never attended a regular chapel or church service, especially in prisons. I saw thousands come to the Lord in these meetings, as I ministered all over the country. There were many times when every person in attendance made an outward commitment to follow the Lord.

Over the years I was one of those believers, a born-again Christian who thought I could use my martial arts experience to minister the pure gospel of Jesus, to win souls by using Karate as a tool. It did appear on the surface that

God approved the use of my talents and expertise, as I saw so many make a profession of faith. When the Lord reveals the fruit of my efforts, only then will I know the numbers of real converts who went on to become more than a statistic. There may have been those who said the "sinner's prayer" for the moment to get a surface relief, but with no lasting commitment to serve the Lord. There may have been those who were possibly moved more by the "experience" of the martial arts demonstration, than by the gospel truth that would set them eternally free.

I may never know how effective or lasting the effect of my preaching was, and that is okay. At the time, I was doing what I knew to do, but I pray that my efforts were not totally futile, and that many survived. I saw all the people come forward so that I could proudly chalk them up as "trophies" of how effective I was in seeking, convincing, and converting them to accept the salvation message. Even though I was a forerunner in using my martial arts experience to evangelize (as many others are now trying to do) I now realize I may have done more harm than good.

It has been a very hard and bumpy road at times that I know I could not have walked down myself, had it not been for God's great mercy and grace. I made mistakes and messes along the way like so many others, but He was there to turn my failures into victories, and my messes into miracles. He used every good and bad circumstance one can imagine in order to turn my life in the right direction.

At the time, the Lord used me for His glory in spite of the deception the enemy still had in that area of my life. You may ask, "How could that be?" I've asked that question, too. I believe it was because my heart was for lost souls, and the anointing and the call on my life as an evangelist had always been there. It had never been removed. God knew I would eventually come all the way out of martial arts! I don't know if these people were sincerely converted or not—only God knows if they were truly transformed by the hearing and preaching of His Word.

We can boast about how great we think we are and about all our accomplishments, but in the final analysis, did we hear and obey the will of the Lord? Did we fight the good fight of faith, or fail to fight the temptations of the world? Were we victorious, or did we become victims? Did we run the race well, or did we get sidetracked? Are we fulfilling the plan and purpose we were created for, or are we giving up and ready to crash and burn? Will the words, "Well done, good and faithful servant," be our final epitaph? Or, will we hear the words, "Depart from Me, you workers of iniquity?" (Luke 13:27)

I have long since repented and have asked God for forgiveness for my ignorance and arrogance in doing what I thought was the right thing, with the right motive and purpose. I pray that God's mercies be extended to those who may have been led to Christ in the wrong way, and that He would redeem them to true salvation. Now, I want to use my testimony to reveal openly my love of the Lord Jesus Christ and the work that He has done in my life. I have yielded my life and my will to Him and allowed Him full access to re-shape, re-mold, and make me into a pure, sanctified vessel that He can work in and through.

Before I got completely out of Karate (the second time), I went on to become a 5-time gold medal winner in national competitions. Unfortunately, there were those who idolized my accomplishments, including members of the church. Eventually there came a day, as I still had my gi and my medals sitting on the floor of my closet, that the Holy Spirit spoke to my heart and said, "How long are you going to keep those?"

That particular day just happened to be Halloween. I had ignored his gentle prompting for some time, but that day seemed to be appropriate for getting rid of any and all attachments I had in my life that still connected me to the martial arts. My wife and I took these items out to our back yard, which happened to be a private wooded area, and I burned every single item. I had been out of the martial arts for quite some time, but that day I completely closed the door on my martial arts involvement once and for all. There was a new level of freedom I received that day and I was able to walk in from that day forward!

To back up a bit, shortly before I had won the gold medals, I decided to walk away from the ministry God had called me to. My reason was because it seemed no one was willing to support the ministry or help me with Christian materials for the new converts. At this time, I developed a video and a program that could help people learn self-defense techniques, which could potentially help them in the event of a possible attacker. As I mentioned before, I had produced a 30-minute film called, "More Than a Fighting Chance." Through the years, I had made many connections with schools, corporate executives, and other groups, and had laid extensive groundwork for this project to take off. But God stopped it through a series of divine interventions in my life. Although I had good (even noble) intentions, God was not in it. It was not His plan—it was my plan!

He finally got my full attention as He brought about extreme circumstances in my life and proceeded to "cut me back to a stump." There are those who might say, "God is not like that." I would say to you: Don't underestimate what God will orchestrate in your life in order to get your full attention! In the natural, I lost everything I had—even my freedom. God brought down my pride once and for all. But through it all, I learned obedience, became humble, and gained knowledge of my true identity in Him.

> But through it all, I learned obedience, became humble, and gained knowledge of my true identity in Him.

His Word began to open up to me like never before as He shared His revelation knowledge, and I began to share it with others. He said if I would obey, He would restore seven-fold everything I had lost. I assure you, He did keep his promise!

May the testimony of my experience reach far and wide, and may many, by the grace of God, learn and turn from anything that is unrighteous and contrary to the will and the Word of God. As you can see, deception and empowerment by demonic forces had kept me blind and in the bondage of pride, anger, and violence, along with a host of other things, from which it took years to be totally set free. My conversion to Christ was real and instantaneous, but my life's baggage was still there. I didn't know how to shake it off. It was like sticky glue. I would partially get it off me and it would bounce back on me. It was an on-going struggle for many years because I had gone back to the very thing God had delivered me out of.

My life had been conformed to Karate, as well as all the bondage that came with it. The shackles were heavy that controlled my life. Karate had been my identity and my life. And it revolved around an occult practice that took years to fully identify and break totally free from. *The enemy of my soul had effectively stolen my new identity in Christ—at least temporarily! But after the Lord got my full attention, He patiently showed me that my identity was in Him and Him alone.* He has restored my true identity in Him and the destiny He had always had in mind for me.

Today, as I look back at all the events that took place in my life, *my only regret is that I didn't listen and obey sooner.* But as Romans 8:28 reminds me, "All things work together for good to those who love God, to those who are called according to His purpose."

CHAPTER 8

ARE MARTIAL ARTS AND CHRISTIANITY COMPATIBLE?

NOT ONLY HAS MARTIAL ARTS become acceptable in mainstream society these days, but, unfortunately, more and more the martial arts (as well as yoga) in various forms are being introduced and accepted into many Christian denominations and churches. This has happened especially in the last decade. Whether they call themselves Baptist, Catholic, Pentecostal, or whatever, it doesn't seem to matter. Is there any place for these activities in a Christian's life? Is there anything about these eastern-related activities that is Christlike? Are these activities that we should have in our churches?

Twenty years ago if someone would have told me that these arts would be incorporated as activities in the church, I would have thought that was ludicrous—that it would never happen! Never say "never." It's happening. Today it has been accepted and made palatable to many believers and leaders alike. What has happened is unthinkable—even unimaginable! It has become a reality for many churches of nearly all denominations and faiths.

This movement toward bringing it into the Judeo-Christian faith primarily started when implemented by the YMCA (Young Men's Christian Association), who have long since divested their Christian roots. It has also been brought in by the JCCs (Jewish Community Centers). Others across the nation would follow suit. Although I had seen the implementation and promotion of the martial arts and yoga in these two organizations, I would never have imagined them moving into the mainstream of both small and major church denominations. Because the YMCA brought martial arts in early on, many thought there was nothing spiritually detrimental in becoming involved. Many went to their pastors or other leaders and suggested: "Why don't we bring it into the church as an evangelistic tool? The YMCA has promoted it, so it must be an acceptable activity for Christians and Jews." And so it became accepted.

In recent years, there has been a phenomenal explosion in the numbers of people practicing what they call "Christian" Karate, Tae Kwon Do, Kung Fu, yoga, etc. This movement has even proliferated to the point that large "so-called" Christian organizations have been formed, such as "Gospel Martial Arts Union," "U. S. Christian Martial Arts Association," and "Karate for Christ International," to name a few. In order to do that, they had to twist Scripture and take it out of context in the most bizarre way! Doing so does not make it biblically correct or justifiable.

I did not begin to realize the extent of the proliferation of these activities into Christian arenas until I bought a newspaper a few years ago. I was at the airport waiting for my plane to depart. I stopped by a newsstand and picked up a "USA Today." I read with casual interest until I came across an article in The Forum section with a bold headline called, "Body & Soul." This article grabbed my full attention, especially as I read the large print under the title. I blurted out loudly in the airport waiting room, "No way!" I startled a few people around me—including myself—which was evident as people turned to stare at me.

The article began with large print as follows: "These days, faith isn't just about paving the path to the afterlife. It's about running trails. It's about yoga. It's about Karate. It's about physical and spiritual health."[1] What caught my full attention was what was sandwiched between running trails and spiritual health—Karate and yoga. I thought, *Where are they going with this article?* I thought for a brief moment, *Okay, why didn't they include seances, fortune telling, and palm reading? Why leave them out?* I proceeded to read the rest of the article, which raised the hair on the back of my neck.

This article went on to say that "a broad-based movement is emerging that wants to reclaim the ancient biblical truth that spirituality involves more than just the spirit—it also includes the body. Links are now being made between faith and fitness in churches and synagogues, Karate schools and yoga studios."[2]

There is no doubt there are links and, to me, they are very apparent. More and more people of faith have become involved in both Karate and yoga, and in turn, are influencing their congregations with the same spirit connected to all martial arts and yoga practices, which is, as I have repeatedly stated, connected with the religions of Hinduism, Buddhism, and Zen.

But the Judeo-Christian faith is obviously not of the same religious root system as the three I just mentioned, therefore, cannot be mixed unless we want to allow spiritual pollution. To do so would be nothing less than spiritual adultery and idolatry. All across America, there is an on-going assault, an undermining of faith, in order to weaken and try to destroy the Judeo-Christian faith from the inside out. Martial arts and yoga are only a part of that widespread assault, which compromises the integrity of one's spiritual wellbeing and brings much defilement.

Again, quoting the article, it said, "Across the USA, congregations are building full-service fitness facilities, expanding the approach pioneered by the YMCAs and JCCs."[3] This approach, supposedly based on faith-based principles, draws people in who otherwise would never consider it. Unfortunately, this approach has worked very well. It appeals to people because it incorporates a so-called sport, as well as exercise-oriented activities, along with the spiritual aspect. Sounds good on the surface... but let's investigate a little further.

There is a package of goods that is being sold to unsuspecting buyers. On the outside of the package, they are told of the so-called benefits on the inside. Common sense tells us to know what we are purchasing. Buyer, beware! Examine the product thoroughly. Know before you buy!

Often people buy on impulse based on promises and/or hype, or simply because something has become very trendy and popular.

Today, this disturbing trend has made inroads into many churches of all denominations, who have blindly invited it in. All one has to do is type in "Christian martial arts" on any search engine. When I did that recently on Google, I got an astounding 8,640,000 results! (I realize many of those are duplicates, but that is still an unbelievable number!) There are those who would say, "See, look at all the sites, the churches, and the ministries that promote Christian Karate and yoga. It must be okay! There is nothing wrong with my becoming involved—besides, it's very popular!"

I wholeheartedly agree that we need to have good exercise programs and healthy eating habits. Obesity and sedentary lifestyles are destroying people, robbing them of their quality of life, or even cutting short their life—not to mention being one of the causes of soaring health care costs. By being proactive, one can prevent many health problems. *But the goal of being physically healthy should not be accomplished by becoming involved in something that would be spiritually detrimental or destructive.*

Many churches across America and around the world have shifted their central focus from being Christ-centered to being "program-centered." The "program-centered" road, in many cases, is a wide road full of road hazards. Or, many try to take two roads at the same time, and this is also a very dangerous trend—more deadly than obesity, sedentary lifestyles, or health issues. *It is spiritual adultery*—trying to walk two roads at the same time, attempting to serve two masters.

It is also idolatry, with self on the throne. After all, *the martial arts is all about self*—self-confidence, self-reliance, self-knowledge, self-sufficiency, self-defense, as well as exaltation of one's ability and accomplishments. That mindset equates to trusting in self, or put another way, a lack of trust in God. It also fuels one's ego and self-importance.

By now, you might be saying, "Vito, what in the world are you talking about?" You might be saying, "I am practicing my Judeo-Christian faith. I attend church all the time, or I am a pastor or elder in my church.

I am sold out to the Lord; our church is growing and healthy. I am not embracing or worshiping other gods or practicing a false religion!"

When a leader in a church allows the martial arts or yoga (under any name) into their church, they are committing *spiritual malpractice!* They are either deceived or in denial, or both! Before you throw my book across the room, please allow me to explain! Many have been blindsided and don't even know it.

If a poisonous snake bit you, you would know immediately. But on the other hand, if you or your family were administered deadly poison in a pleasant drink, a little at a time, you wouldn't know what happened until sickness or death occurred. You might not even make the connection as to the cause. I call it *death by stealth*—blinded and poisoned one degree at a time. It will first weaken, then spiritually debilitate, and can eventually destroy that person.

Sound impossible? Well, it is possible and happening every day to thousands of people from all faiths, in hundreds of churches. Online there is way more information that I can possibly write about in one book regarding the martial arts and yoga and how these activities have crept into Judeo/Christianity. Let's look at just a few successful intrusions into churches that were mentioned in another article of USA Today called "Fitness & Faith." I quote as follows:

- Parkwood Baptist Church in Annandale, Virginia offers "Christian Yoga" for people to get in shape and connect with God. The unity of mind and body embraced by yoga practitioners is an attractive dimension of this ancient Hindu spiritual practice, as is its promise of stronger muscles, improved flexibility, and stress relief.[4]

- "Body & Soul," a fitness ministry with classes in 29 states and 16 countries conducts sessions in aerobics and strength training set to Christian music. It advertises itself as the place where faith and fitness meet.[5]

- The physical strength, coordination, and self-knowledge promised by the martial arts have made classes in Karate and Tae Kwon Do popular.

The organization "Karate for Christ International" offers a Christian-based experience.[6]

Notice the words "self-knowledge." The promotion of self-knowledge (which often includes self-awareness, through the practice of meditation) is nothing less than an introduction to the religions of Hinduism and/or Zen Buddhism. The New Age practices (which are nothing less than warmed-over Hinduism) have now been made palatable and easier to swallow. The comment in the above article, "connect with God," begs an answer to the question, "Which god?" And "What faith are we talking about here?" "What music?" How does the martial arts give one a Christ-centered experience? *This is an abortion of truth!*

Today we are experiencing an unprecedented movement that incorporates the martial arts (as a physical fitness and self-defense activity) and yoga practices (to supposedly learn to meditate in order to grow closer to God) in churches around the world. Joseph Agius (a former martial artist) asked this question and gives his answer, to which I concur:

> Is Christianity and martial arts compatible? I am sure that many say they are, while others say they are not. I have to approach the matter with great care because in no way do I want to personally attack those who are in the view that Christianity and martial arts are compatible...My position is a definite "no." They do not agree.[7]

Speaking of my own experience now, since I have been on both sides of the issue (and now have come all the way out) I clearly know the difference. I know why not to be involved any longer, and I know what is deceiving and empowering those who are. From my own perspective, having had the experience and background that I have, I can adamantly say that the concept of "Christian martial arts" is an oxymoron if there ever was one. We cannot serve two masters at the same time. It will not work. I tried and failed miserably, as many others have. You see, martial arts and yoga are both very spiritual activities—*but not everything that is spiritual is of God!*

Again, quoting from online:

Although some proponents for a "Christian" martial arts do concede that Karate has roots in occult, pagan, and/or eastern religious philosophy, they also claim that the primary philosophy behind the martial arts actually originated in Old Testament Biblical times (citing such passages as Genesis 14:13-16; Second Samuel 6:14; Psalm 144:1; and Ecclesiastes 9:10 as proof-texts), even going back all the way to the Garden of Eden! (Christian Martial Arts, Tottingham & Tottingham, pp. v & 2).

Therefore, according to these advocates, Satan made "inroads" into the true Bible-based martial arts, capturing them for himself, and that all we need to do now is to reclaim them and change them "from an Asiatic philosophy to a truly Bible-centered Christian philosophy" (Christian Martial Arts, pp. ii & 2). Once these "dramatic changes" in "approach" are made, we are told, the "Christian can indeed study the martial arts in total harmony with his walk with the Lord" (Christian Martial Arts, p. v).[8]

What deception! Yet, many have believed that one, and it is a very dangerous philosophy. The same article goes on to refute it in this way:

This, of course, is the same logic men use to "Christianize" any worldly, pagan, and/or occult philosophy or practice, whether it be astrology (the "Gospel in the Stars"), psychology, eastern "medicine," magic, pyramidology, graphology, numerology, etc., etc., etc. The logic goes something like this: "It was originated by God (which requires a few verses out of context to prove it), Satan stole it and/or counterfeited it (under the false assumption that *Satan can't create, he just steals from God*), we need to reclaim it and re-Christian it, and then we can use it to glorify God" (Christian Martial Arts, pp. 75, 83).[9]

I guess we could debate the point whether Satan can create or not. He certainly cannot create in the same way as God, the Creator, but we must acknowledge that Satan has created false religions, doctrines of demons, false philosophies, and certainly everything pertaining to the evil occult realm. He has certainly raised up many false teachers, prophets, and apostles who operate in his devil anointing. The Bible says that

Satan himself is able to masquerade as an angel of light, (according to Second Corinthians 11:14) and by doing so, has and will continue to deceive many who do not love the truth or seek the truth.

In First John 5:19, the Bible tells us that "the whole world lies under the sway of the wicked one." If we, as Christians, partake of the activities of the world (such as martial arts and yoga), we give the wicked one the legal right to bring us under his influence! In order to come out from under that influence, we must first make a quality decision not to partake of these kinds of things, and if we already have, we must be willing to give them up in order to be free.

The greatest deception of all is that many in the church have openly embraced these ancient arts instead of coming out! They have somehow become convinced that by changing their names, playing Christian music, praying, or calling it "family fun and exercise," they can somehow sanitize them and change the real purpose for which these arts were originally designed. Whatever benefits might be derived are never worth the cost—spiritually speaking! There is an underlying disguise, brought about by seducing spirits, which are deceiving millions of undiscerning people, both Christians and non-Christians alike.

Martial arts and yoga instructors have infiltrated the church at large and have convinced untold thousands of church-going believers in Christ that these activities can be "cleaned up." The false concept is that they can *safely embrace and enjoy the benefits* of them, because of their new "sanitized" methods of instruction, which no longer have any connection to any undesirable spiritual aspect! The lie is that one can disinfect it as one might do using a sanitizer on the handles of a shopping cart in a grocery store.

Unfortunately, these instructors have already enjoyed a large measure of success in attaching Christ's name to these eastern arts and practices. But what "Jesus" is attached to occult activities? Would Jesus of Nazareth use or promote any of these practices, which are fully connected to Hinduism, Buddhism, and Zen? Would He have allowed the violence that is connected to the martial arts, or the meditation practices (of both yoga and martial arts) that allow spiritual connection and participation into a demonic realm to operate in His life?

Absolutely not! Does praying, using Christian music, attaching Christ's name to the activity, or putting a cross on the back of a uniform protect the Christian from the extreme dangers and seducing spirits that are connected to all of these arts? No! How can one possibly separate the practices of martial arts and/or yoga from the occult—and Christianize them? It is possible for a person to become purified and sanctified by the power of the Holy Spirit, but it is impossible to sanctify any object or activity that is rooted in the occult—that which God has adamantly forbidden!

It is possible for a person to become purified and sanctified by the power of the Holy Spirit, but it is impossible to sanctify any object or activity that is rooted in the occult–that which God has adamantly forbidden!

Would there not be a spirit of antichrist that is attached to these occult religions, which are birthed, influenced, and controlled by satanic forces? These religions have existed for thousands of years and have tried to exert their influence over the people of God centuries ago. As an example, look at the children of Israel, who were delivered out of bondage from Egypt—a place of both physical and spiritual slavery. They were warned by God through Moses not to associate with those who participated in these kinds of activities, not to participate themselves, not to intermarry with those who did, and not to even have any objects in their possessions that were occult-related, lest they be accursed. If something was conceived in the womb of occult meditation and brought through the birth canal of false religions, shouldn't we, as Christians, avoid it like the plague?

If something was conceived in the womb of occult meditation and brought through the birth canal of false religions, shouldn't we, as Christians, avoid it like the plague?

Many times these occult religions have remained to themselves, not trying to exert any influence over any of those in any other belief system. But today, there is an all-out effort to infiltrate, pervert, and/or convert, those of the Judeo-Christian faith by bringing in a very dangerous, ungodly mixture. The Bible warns us that these things will happen, especially in the last days. It says that the spirit of antichrist will arise, declaring all kinds of falsehoods, whose ultimate goal is to deceive even "the elect," if possible (See Matthew 24:24).

The questions that should be asked are these: "Why does a Christian need the martial arts or yoga in his life? Why is it being blindly accepted into the church?" The way I see it, what has influenced believers in Christ to accept these arts into their churches is no mystery. It has originated from within the church, not from without!

> *It has originated from within the church, not from without!*

It has come in from those who are already leaders and/or members of various congregations. The position of influence of certain members of these churches has allowed them to be the vehicle by which the enemy has been, and is being, allowed to infiltrate. Some of these people were already involved in eastern religious practices before they became believers, just as I was. Some in the church are already martial arts instructors or students, and simultaneously have a title or position in the church as well.

Sometimes they are simply looking for space for a dojo, and they may ask permission to use the church facility. They have inadvertently been allowed to bring in this kind of influence simply because they are already a member, or operating from a trusted position of influence. Others (who may never have been involved in the martial arts, and therefore, have little or no knowledge about it) have become convinced that it can be used as an evangelistic tool.

As a result of inviting these activities into the church and onto the church grounds, the church body itself has become greatly compromised. Many individuals who are church goers, even though they made a stand

for Christ, never got set free from the powers which had been controlling certain areas of their lives, as a result of their own previous involvement. Therefore, the baggage they retained, and the deceptive influence
that they are still under, is brought into their Christian faith (and/or the
church) because it is still a part of who they are.

The same could be said of those who have been involved in freemasonry, witchcraft, etc. The effects of being involved, especially in occult
activities, can be far-reaching in one's life, and tenaciously hang on after
one becomes a Christian. That is why there must be a deep cleansing or
purging of the effects of these activities in order for believers to walk in
freedom, power, and total victory. As I mentioned earlier, for many who
were involved in the martial arts, their identity is so wrapped up in that
entire experience that they often don't readily want to give it up.

Instead, they try very hard to Christianize it, claiming all sorts of things
that simply are not true, including using Scripture out of context to try
to defend their position—what I call the "cut and paste" approach. This
approach never works because we must understand Scripture in its whole
context in order to rightly interpret it. There are many versions of the argu-
ments for promoting these activities, and I do believe I have heard them all.

I repeat, people are trying to walk down two roads at the same time. At
the very least, there is still a mixture. This is what the apostle Paul referred
to as "leaven" in the church. In First Corinthians 5:6 he asked this question,
"Do you not know that a little leaven leavens the whole lump?" In Verse
7, he says, "Therefore, purge out the old leaven, that you may be a new
lump." In essence, what he is saying is that old ungodly habits and practices,
as well as strongholds, must be removed before a Christian believer can
truly walk in newness of life. If this is not done, it will begin to affect the
entire church. And I'm not just talking about martial arts and yoga here!

Martial arts frequently comes into the church in one of three main
ways: 1) under the guise of physical fitness, 2) promoted as a need for
self-defense, or 3) as an evangelistic outreach. It comes in, as I said,
through individuals who usually are sincere and have noble intentions,

but simply lack knowledge and discernment about what is behind every single form of martial arts and yoga! Ignorance is not bliss, nor is it an excuse. Let's look at each of these three reasons.

Physical fitness – It is touted as a good way to have fun, bring families together, and get physically fit all at the same time. As I have stated before, there are so many other ways to become physically fit without the adverse spiritual ramifications that are part and parcel of the martial arts. I was in the best physical shape I could possibly be in when I was involved, but that physical conditioning covered up two things:

1. Injuries that were not apparent at the time and would not show up until years later. By that time, cartilage and bone damage was so far advanced that it would have been nearly impossible to repair without extensive surgery, or a healing miracle by God.

2. My spiritual condition was well hidden and actually didn't surface fully until the realization that there were forces operating in me and controlling much of my everyday life. (I have already shared how I got free from those forces.)

In the practice of all martial arts, the goal is to learn how to overpower another person. This cannot help but produce an attitude of aggression and violence! How can punching, kicking, and throwing another human being down produce a graceful, humble, peaceful spirit in a person? It cannot possibly produce the fruit of the Spirit of God in a person's life.

All that it produces—violence, anger, pride, aggression, etc.—is the diametric opposite of Christlikeness. One cannot walk into any dojo or gym (whether it claims to be Christian or not) without sensing the uneasiness of the spiritual atmosphere. The very nature of these violent forms of expressions runs counter to God's Word.

Self-defense – Initially, it may sound like a good argument and it is good to be protective of one's life and one's family. It is also a good idea to use precaution and not purposely expose oneself to danger. But in all my years of involvement, I have never had to use my expertise to defend myself out on the street. Although there were a number of occasions that could have escalated into violence, I was able to diffuse the situation instead. An instance of a martial artist having to defend him or herself out on the streets is very rare indeed.

Now I have heard of plenty of times when they wanted to test their skills and provoked a fight, but that's not the same as self-defense, is it? If any person is determined enough as an attacker to go after a weaker person, he usually has enough experience to accomplish his goal. As I said before, if a person has never had to actually defend him or herself in an unknown condition or circumstance, that person would be at a tremendous disadvantage, especially if the attacker is armed with a weapon, or if there are multiple attackers involved.

In the supervised, controlled environment of the dojo, there is no "element of surprise." Everyone knows what to expect. I know instructors and high-level students who were well trained in the martial arts, but simply did not trust their abilities on the street, and several admitted that they carried guns or other weapons to protect themselves. The very fear they were trying to overcome was obviously still present!

In action scenes depicting self-defense in the movies, one often sees a person defending him or herself against other individuals or multiple attackers, many of them with weapons. What most people don't know is that not all of the attackers actually attack all at once. It is one by one and in slow motion. But when the film is edited, it is sped up to make it exciting, like it is all happening at full speed everywhere at once. Because of this kind of Hollywood hype and delusions of grandeur, many believe that they can get involved in the martial arts and simply become like supermen.

Many demonstrations and exhibitions are held in schools, parks, malls, and in churches where instructors and/or students are trying to impress people with their skills, entice them to join their particular club, or show them their "so-called" need for self-defense. These are planned and precisely choreographed moves so that everything comes off perfectly and no one is injured. If anyone deviates from the plan, or if one of the participants suddenly changes something from the original plan, somebody can be seriously injured. If that were to happen, they certainly would not be able to accomplish their intended purpose, which is to convince as many viewers as possible that they could benefit from this training.

Many times people want to learn martial arts because of their own fear of crime and violence and the perceived need to protect oneself and one's family. If we, as Christians, need to be in charge of our own "self-defense," are we not saying that we are self-sufficient in that sense, and don't need God to protect and defend us with His holy angels?

A well-known story that happened many years ago was the story of David Wilkerson, meeting up on the street with notoriously violent gang leader, Nicky Cruz. Nicky had a bad reputation on the streets of doing great bodily harm with a knife. Reputation had it that Nicky never missed! The day David found himself face to face with Nicky Cruz was a day that changed two lives forever. As David tried to share the gospel, Nicky tried repeatedly to stab David. But not once was he even able to get near him, as David was protected with what appeared to be a solid shield—an unseen force of angelic protection.

David wasn't in the wrong place at the wrong time, but, as it turned out, he was exactly where God wanted him. As a result of that encounter, Nicky found a greater power—that of Jesus Christ—and he gave his life to the Lord on the spot! He went on to become an evangelist, and I would imagine that David's faith soared to a whole new level that day. Not only that, but many are still being inspired by hearing this story, through the book and the movie that followed, *The Cross and the Switchblade*. As a result of this "God encounter," Nicky's testimony is still reaching thousands. He is not using his knife anymore, but now he uses a sword—the Word of God!

In another story, the infamous South Side rapist of St. Louis, Missouri, Dennis Rabbitt, had successfully raped countless women for well over a decade. After he was finally caught in New Mexico and was being interrogated by the police, he admitted to all the rapes he had committed. He was only being investigated for rapes committed for about a ten-year period, but he actually admitted to raping around 100 women altogether, over a much longer period of time. He stated, however, that there was one woman he was not able to rape. She stopped him in his tracks because she used the name of Jesus! Now that's power! No other "self-defense" needed!

There was another story a few years ago of a young man who was a former star college football player. One day he went on a rampage and shot at a few people. Twelve police officers tried every way they knew how to subdue him. They finally tasered him and beat him, and still he was overpowering all of them. Almost all police officers have to have self-defense training—but that day, none of their training helped. They finally had to shoot and kill him because he was totally out of control.

Imagine one trained just in self-defense trying to defend himself against a person like that. There are many cases, too numerous to mention, of even skilled martial artists who have failed against determined violent attackers. So, how can we fathom that young children or women (or men) can effectively defend themselves against a person intent on doing great bodily harm?

Evangelistic Outreach - Based on presumption and a lack of knowledge, many in the church believe that martial arts can be used as an evangelistic outreach, to win souls to Jesus Christ. (As we know, He is the Truth, the Light, and the Prince of Peace.) *So how can we use an activity based on occult practices, rooted in false religions, and seeped in violence to win people to Jesus?* I now call it "reverse evangelism." It's evangelism all right, but the enemy's purposes are, more often than not, being served by it. I believe people are often being drawn to the "spirit of the martial arts" and the excitement of seeing a demonstration, rather than being moved by the Spirit of God through love and compassion.

The enemy's strategies and methods of warfare have not changed. He is skillfully infiltrating and executing his clandestine plan, not just from the outside anymore, but now from the inside—where he is being much more effective. The body of Christ (the organic church) is the greatest prize (other than the throne of God) that the enemy, "the dragon," is trying to overthrow and conquer.

Sadly, in some cases, he seems to be conquering without much of a fight, because many are cooperating with him, rather than resisting him. At the very least, he has been allowed to weaken the church in many areas. There are dragons in some pulpits and his helpers in the pews. Hosea 4:6 says, "My people perish for lack of knowledge."

Many Christians and churches are throwing caution to the wind, and are about to reap the dire consequences, if they haven't already, because they failed to "test the spirit(s)," as we are told to do in First John 4:1-6. No one is immune. Once that door is opened, the invisible demonic forces will jump for joy that you have allowed them to take up residence in your life, or in the life of your church, without even a fight.

There are those who might say, "Well, the Bible does not specifically say that we should not practice martial arts or yoga." An article I read online from a Christian perspective has this to say in response:

> The Lord Jesus Christ did not fight nor teach His immediate disciples (or His future followers) how to fight physically in the three and a half years He walked physically with them. If it had been as important to defend one-self physically (as some try to persuade us) even in those robber-infested roads of Jericho, surely the Grandest Master who ever walked the earth (or will walk the earth) would have taught a few basic joint locks and kicks, etc! On the contrary, He taught self-sacrifice, blessing and loving one's enemies, and submitting the rest of our situations, circumstances, and outcomes to God, who is ever watching over His own, and will surely defend them.[10]

Several have tried to justify their involvement in martial arts by twisting Scriptures. Some might try to use the story in Luke 4:28-30, saying that when the angry mob was trying to throw Jesus off a cliff, He was able to walk through them because of His great martial arts techniques. Here is how the Bible account reads:

So all those in the synagogue, when they heard these things, were filled with wrath, and rose up and thrust Him out of the city; and they led Him to the brow of the hill on which their city was built, that they might throw Him down over the cliff. Then passing through the midst of them, He went His way.

Luke 4:28-30

There are those who might try to use the biblical account of this scenario to justify their involvement. They might say that when Jesus got "pushed to the limit," He puffed himself up like Arnold Schwarzenegger, and then He contorted his face, and screamed like Bruce Lee. Then to really demonstrate His power, they might say, He set up some concrete blocks, and with a mighty scream smashed the blocks to smithereens.

Then they might add that He stood up, walked through the crowd, methodically deflecting the blows that were coming at Him from every direction, as He made His way out of town. That is ludicrous, to say the least! It's amazing to me how people twist the Scriptures to support what their flesh wants to do, rather than rightly dividing the Word of truth and dying to their fleshly desires that take them away from God!

Let's look at another scenario with Jesus and see the real power that He possessed without lifting a finger. John 18:3-6 tells us that Judas came with an entire detachment of troops and officers from the chief priests and Pharisees, and that they had lanterns, torches, and weapons. When Jesus asked them whom they were seeking, they told Him, "Jesus of Nazareth." Verse 5 tells us that Jesus answered them and said, "I am He." When He uttered those powerful words, Verse 6 tells us, "They drew back and fell to the ground." Now that's real power!

In the Matthew 26:47-56 (NIV) account of the same scenario, when Jesus was confronted by those who had come to arrest Him, Simon Peter (yielding to what his flesh prompted him to do) pulled out his sword and cut off the right ear of the servant of the high priest. In response, Jesus touched his ear and healed him right on the spot. Then Jesus made a very significant statement as He told Peter in Verse 52: "Put your sword back in its place...for all who draw the sword will die by the sword." There are those who practice martial arts incorporating the use of various weapons, such as the sword, the seih, the nunchaku, and others, who are, in essence, taking the spirit of violence to another level. Jesus is the Prince of Peace—quite the opposite of violence!

Some would say, "Well, we have a right to defend ourselves." Yes, you do. You have the right to do anything you want. *But when we decide to take matters into our own hands, we can forfeit the protection that would have been there for us.* The angels of God have been assigned to protect true believers. If we throw caution to the wind and make wrong choices, we will always reap bad consequences. Many times, we simply need to use common sense to stay away from undesirable or dangerous situations and places.

However, that is not always possible. There have been times I have been tested to the max. I have been in circumstances where some very violent and determined men, who for no reason, wanted to attack me. I stood my ground and was determined not to rely on my former martial arts experience and expertise. Instead, I trusted the Lord completely.

They were not able to penetrate a three-foot area that completely surrounded me. It was as if I had an invisible bubble of protection around me. Even though they were coming at me with vile language and gestures, they could not touch me in any way. As suddenly as it all started, it was as though they felt or sensed a power greater than their own and chose to back up and not proceed with their intent. I was amazed to see the protection of the angels of the Lord around me! Now some might say that my attackers sensed my confidence and that is what caused them to back away. Yes, but it wasn't my self-confidence—it was my confidence that the Lord would protect me!

Why would a Christian spend time developing carnal, physical weapons when the actual warfare against us is spiritual in nature? God has given us divinely powerful spiritual weapons that will literally bring down any evil spirits that are arrayed against us (if we are walking in truth and obedience). How many have forfeited the truth and sold themselves to the dragon's cunning lies!

That dragon of old is quite content as long as we are wrapped up in the natural and physical realm and never mature enough, as Christians, to exercise the proper use of our spiritual weapons. I'm talking about the greatest power in the universe—the name of Jesus and the authority and power He Himself gave us to "bind" the power of evil spirits (in His name).

Believers need a revelation of the truth, understanding of what has been allowed to take place in their Christian walk, and in the church. *Discernment needs to be first and foremost, but for many, deception has already come, because they loved not the truth, that they might be spared from deception and delusion.* (See Second Thessalonians 2:10-11.) It will take an awakening for the church to see that their enemy is hell-bent on their destruction and has been allowed to invade and control their lives from within. Piece by piece, many have been losing ground to evil unseen forces without even knowing it.

For example, Billy Blanks (who claims to be a Christian believer) has introduced martial arts through his "Tae Bo Believer's Workout" DVD. One website, which advertises this DVD, claims that one can experience "the pure inspirational power of Tae Bo,"[11] and can "achieve a truly amazing transformation of the body and mind."[12] There is certainly nothing pure about the martial arts in any form, and why would we want martial arts, which is rooted in the occult, to be the tool we use to transform our minds?

The advertisement goes on to say, "When you first exercise your will, your physical body comes along with it. When these two work in harmony, the result is strength far greater than any mere workout can achieve. And Billy's pure motivation – backed up by the Lord just can't be beat."[13]

Nonsense! First of all, this is the same subtle logic that those who claim to be "Christian martial artists" use to entice others to join their dojos or programs. From a Christian standpoint, this logic is severely flawed. We cannot gain a "strength far greater" unless it comes from a supernatural spiritual source. The question, again, is which source? If we are connecting a physical "workout" to anything rooted in the martial arts, the supernatural strength we gain will definitely be from the wrong spiritual source. There are only two sources of supernatural strength or power—from God or from Satan. As a Christian, which one do you desire?

Christian television and Christian magazines also promote the martial arts and yoga. On May 10th, 2008, TBN aired a program, featuring Carman, the popular Christian vocalist. He invited some high-profile pastors (one being Dr. Christian Harfouche) as well as competitors who were involved in mixed martial arts, to be on his program. These men boldly proclaimed they were masters in the martial arts, flaunting their abilities on the program.

This kind of thing certainly entices other Christians to become involved. It is very dangerous to use one's platform or fame in the church community to promote deception, causing people to go down the wrong road, but it's not my place to judge them. What they do is between them and God. As believers, however, we are required to test, examine, and appraise the doctrinal integrity of a minister's message, as well as examine the fruit of his character, to see whether it lines up with the Word of God. Ephesians 5:11 (NAS) tells us: "Do not participate in the unfruitful deeds of darkness, but instead expose them."

I was attending a conference a few years ago in the Midwest, and Dr. Harfouche (from Pensacola, Florida) was one of a number of speakers. (A couple of our minister friends were also speaking, so we went primarily to hear them speak.) I didn't know anything about this pastor from Florida, but when he stood up to speak, something troubled me that I could not shake. I was discerning something about him that was not Christlike because I sensed so much pride and control emanating from him. I was thoroughly disgusted, as were many others who were sitting around me, who outwardly complained about the manipulative methods he was using to try to get a big offering. One woman behind us even said, "We want to give, but not like this!" (By the way, the Bible tells us not to give under compulsion, but rather of our own free will.)

In the spring of 2008, I just happened to be speaking at a spiritual warfare conference in Tampa about how the martial arts have crept into the church. There I met a pastor who told me that Dr. Harfouche was scheduled to appear in a couple of months on Carman's program, which was to be about the martial arts. Only then did I make the connection from when I first saw him at the conference in the Midwest.

I now understood what I had been discerning all along, which was operating in him. It was the spirits behind the martial arts—pride, arrogance, and control. At the time, I was stunned by his arrogance, and now I know why. I was discerning much deception and evil operating in someone who was presenting himself to be a leader in the body of Christ, a man of God.

After hearing about his appearance on TBN, I decided to check out his website for myself. Once again, I was stunned by what I saw, by what he claimed to be, and how he had intertwined Christianity with martial arts. He touts himself as a grand master and claims to be a world leader in the field of martial arts. He actually has several websites, which I visited.

On one I found an article which was written by one of his students, Jennifer Keating. The article had appeared in the February 2004 edition of Black Belt magazine and was entitled, "The Art of Deception." (Interesting title, wouldn't you say?) Jennifer says that as a youth growing up on the streets of Los Angeles, he was smaller than the average adversary, and that he quickly became skilled in the art of strategic deception because it allowed him to gain an advantage over bigger bullies.

I understand that at that time he had not yet met Jesus, but now that he has (supposedly in 1977), why is he still engaged in this occult practice and claiming to be a grand master in the world of martial arts? Why is he teaching and promoting martial arts? His websites show many pictures of him on the covers of magazines such as "Black Belt," "Tapout," "Gladiator," "Bodyguard," and "Inside Kung Fu." On these covers, he is pictured right alongside very violent-looking people. Check out his site for yourself if you like: www.shoritetaijutso.com.

He is not alone. There are others like him who claim to be Christian, who claim to be representing Jesus Christ, but at the same time are operating in occult practices, again, attempting to serve two masters at the same time.

That's deception. When people are deceived, they are like the blind leading the blind. Jesus said they would both fall into the ditch. (See Matthew 15:14.)

A few years ago, I began hearing about activities going on in synagogues, Roman Catholic churches, and others, that had allowed such things as palm readers, seances, tarot card reading, and New Age practices, by inviting those who practice such activities to come in. I was told by those who were attending these and other church groups that they didn't think these activities did any harm, and besides, they were entertaining and fun, like bingo. *Yeah, right,* I thought, *like bingo!*

Just like the martial arts and yoga, they didn't know that they were participating in occult practices, which God has emphatically told His people not to do! (See Deuteronomy 18:10-11 and Acts 19:19.) The reason God is so emphatic about telling His people not to have contact with the occult spirit realm is because *the forces and beings in that realm are alien and hostile to God! If we are children of God,* that means they are alien and hostile to us as well.

These occult activities I just described were not introduced from the outside, but were introduced by those from other churches, or from influence on the inside. *One might say the enemy had a formal, engraved invitation.* I don't know where these churches and synagogues are today, but I do believe there is a mixed mess that has polluted these congregations—to what degree, only God knows.

Many times these things are allowed into peoples' lives because they are looking for answers. They are searching for truth and power, and maybe not finding it in their church. Or they may find a form of godliness, but no real power, so they inadvertently turn to knowledge and power from the occult realm instead. What a shame! If people do not find the real thing where they are supposed to find it (in the church), the enemy is all too glad to offer his version of knowledge and power, which will always cause one to miss the mark and fall short.

It may even look and sound like the real thing, but it will instead cause a person to be seduced and led astray. The so-called "inner peace, tranquility, and relief from stress" that the yoga instructors tout as benefits may give one a feeling of peacefulness, but it will actually be the devil's counterfeit to the true peace that only comes from knowing Jesus, the Prince of Peace.

Some church leaders have heard about what was being allowed in other churches, and oftentimes these other churches just happened to be headed up by ministers they themselves admired and respected. Some have followed suit simply because they trusted these leaders to be spiritually astute. I have a friend who attends a church of about 6000 in the Midwest. His pastor stood up on a Sunday morning and proudly announced that he was going to allow the martial arts to be taught in his church and that he himself would be participating.

This same pastor, years ago, judged and condemned me for teaching the martial arts, even though I was incorporating Bible study, prayer, and evangelism outreach with it at the time. (Today, as I said in the previous chapter, I question the validity of what I was doing back then.) Yet now, years later, he is allowing the very same thing (which he openly condemned earlier) to come into his own church, with the potential of adversely affecting thousands of lives.

I believe it is possible that he may have been influenced to do so because of a friend (whom he trusted) who is a pastor of another church, which had promoted the martial arts. This pastor in the Midwest is now suffering from some on-going physical ailments, one of which came on him suddenly after he demonstrated a kick from the pulpit one Sunday. Is this a coincidence? I don't think so.

Many other churches are following suit. I attended a conference several years ago that was held in former pastor Ted Haggard's church. At that time, I was discerning a number of things that didn't feel quite right. A few years later, I learned that he also had allowed five different martial arts groups to be in his church, and I know some of them are still in operation, even though he is no longer the pastor. Most people know that he fell from grace and even though that wasn't the reason he fell, many of the devil's works are intertwined and bring a snare through deception and pride.

Another church we ministered at (in the South) had a pastor who was a phenomenal teacher and a wonderful person. He had had his church for six or seven years and could not seem to grow it beyond twenty-five or thirty people. Yet he didn't understand why his church wasn't growing in numbers, nor did I at first. The next day, however, I found out that he had allowed one of his elders (who also happened to be a wonderful man) to have a club called, "Kicking for Jesus," right next door to the church. There could have been other factors as well preventing the growth, but I believe that was certainly one of them.

A vibrant Assembly of God church we attended for a short time decided to start Tae Kwon Do classes and it brought in all kinds of stuff. The next thing we knew they were bringing in evil video games for the teenagers and painting the walls of the video game room black. There was disunity, control, and strife as well. All of this culminated in a strong prophetic word coming forth one Sunday morning in which God declared that the Holy Spirit was departing from that church. When the Holy Spirit departed, we also departed. We really don't want to be where the Holy Spirit is not.

Another church I was a part of (non-denominational) nearly made a fatal mistake, as well. They almost allowed a member of their church to conduct Karate classes, all under the guise of "self-defense." They already had the information printed up in their color brochure, and all was set to go. A member of the church contacted me and informed me that martial arts was about to be taught there, but, at the time, my wife and I were about a week away from moving from Missouri to Florida. I thought, I'm moving shortly and I really don't want to get involved at this time. They know my background and how I feel about the martial arts. If they want to know, they will contact me.

Well, that is exactly what happened a few weeks later, one morning as my wife and I were praying for that church. Two hours later, I received a phone call and was given an opportunity to share with them all the "spiritual" reasons why I would advise anyone against bringing in this activity. They decided to cancel it! I even told them what would happen when they talked to the proposed instructors of this class (a man and his wife) to tell them they had decided to cancel the class. I told them if they were submitted to godly authority, and if their lives were sold out to the Lord, they would be okay with the leadership's decision. And if not, they would respond vehemently, which would expose the ulterior motive—the enemy's intent to infiltrate and pollute their church.

The response was exactly as I thought it would be. The man and his wife were both in the meeting. (They had left their autistic son in the children's care on the floor below where the meeting was.) When they received the news, the wife began to scream "kiai" as loud as she could and ran out of the room. Actually, she was manifesting a demon.

At the exact same moment, her son also began to manifest out of control in the childcare room, which was on a different floor. You can bet the demonic realm thought they had made inroads into this vibrant and fast-growing church! They thought it was a "done deal." Sure enough, the couple did not submit to authority, but instead left the church—possibly taking their plan elsewhere?

There are undesirable consequences for those Christians who decide to participate in the martial arts, and for those who remain in it after they become a Christian. They are as follows:

1. Divination (psychic ability, able to read thoughts and/or project thoughts)
2. Violence / murder / Bushido warrior spirit
3. Supernatural energy, strength, or power called "ch'i" (Chinese) or "ki" (Japanese) - which comes from an evil spirit.
4. Hate / cruelty
5. Aggressiveness / tendency to provoke fights
6. Invincible feeling
7. Intimidation over others (wants others to fear them)
8. Mind control (being controlled and controlling others)
9. Competitiveness and superior attitudes

10. Can become suicidal (fear of being a failure, losing honor, or because of false belief in karma and reincarnation)

11. Pride – arrogance, haughtiness (found in nearly all instructors and students)

12. Idolatry of students toward instructor

13. Control (lording it over others)

14. Conscience is dulled to sin and the need for repentance

15. Self sufficiency; self-will; self-confidence; self-trust

16. Gives a counterfeit identity (which is not Christlike in any way)

17. Self-defense (what about our guardian angels and our authority in the name of Jesus?)

18. Deception (some actually begin to follow after false religions)

19. Sexual temptation because of "touch," etc. (or transference of evil spirits by what amounts to inappropriate intimate touch)

20. Result of yielding to sexual temptation – adultery, fornication, and/or breakup of marriages

21. Stunted in one's growth as a Christian – not able to move forward

22. The spirits behind martial arts are opposite of the "fruit of the Spirit" and block its development and maturity

23. Physical consequences take their toll on one's body

There are also consequences if it is allowed into the church. It can bring in any of the things mentioned earlier for individuals, as well as the following:

1. Potential of lawsuits if someone is injured on the church grounds

2. Seducing spirits of error and deception

3. Spiritual dullness and blindness over the entire church, including leaders

4. Pride and egotism

5. Sorcery (control)

6. Doubt and unbelief

7. Sexual immorality and perverseness

8. Removes the "fear of the Lord" – no talk about sin or repentance

9. Fosters a lack of discernment

10. Quenches the power of the Holy Spirit

11. Lack, poverty, or barrenness (which are effects from occult involvement)

12. Health problems

So, once again, I pose the question, "Does martial arts have any place in a Christian's life?" What could possibly be the scriptural basis for bringing it into the church? Some might quote the apostle Paul from First Corinthians 9:22, "I have become all things to all men, that I might by all means save some." Many have taken this verse quite literally, and in the process, taken it out of context.

If I become all things to all men, does that mean I become a drug dealer, or a prostitute, or a pimp, in order to win people to the Lord? This is no different! Does that mean I go out and cover myself with tattoos and piercings in order to reach gang members? There are some that have, and then declare that they are "under grace." Do I smoke a little dope to win the user over to Christ? Absolutely not! How can we use a tool empowered by the pit of hell to win souls for the kingdom of God?

That is not what Paul meant and that verse has been misconstrued to mean something it doesn't mean, and has never meant. This misinterpretation has given people (in their own minds) a license to operate in both the world and be a Christian at the same time. The apostle Paul went on to say in Romans 12:2 that we are not to "be conformed to this world." And in Second Corinthians 6:17 he says that we are to come out from among those in the world in the way we operate and conduct ourselves.

This is not a plague that has crept in the back door, but one that is being allowed in through the front door of many churches today, an ancient arch-enemy who has not only been allowed, but actually invited to infiltrate the church! The battle lines have clearly been drawn and now more than ever, we have three choices:

1. We can cower in defeat

2. We can do nothing and perish in ignorance

3. Or, we can fight and win (spiritually speaking)

All of the above will cost something. We will not be able to keep everyone happy. What price are we willing to pay? It is our choice. What we tolerate we get to keep. What we ignore has a right to stay and will not go away. What we invite in certainly has a legal right to enter and stay. What we embrace, we will conform to. What we allow into our lives will define and control us.

Proverbs 16:25 puts it like this: "There is a way that seems right to a man, but its end is the way of death." May God give you, the reader, understanding and conviction by His Holy Spirit to depart from unfruitful works of darkness and instead invest your time, energy, resources, and talents to prepare yourself for His Second Coming. He will come suddenly and will judge every man's deeds done in the body, as well as our thoughts and words. Let no one who reads this say he was not warned ahead of time.

For those who are now ready to be free of the bondage of martial arts and yoga, following are prayers of repentance, renunciation, breaking ungodly soul ties, and dismantling the spiritual strongholds. In order to be completely free, one must also be willing to destroy any items associated with the practice of either of these activities. One should not sell or give away any of the objects connected with the martial arts or yoga, whether trophies, garments, or anything used in this practice.

Rather, they should burn them as an outward announcement and open display of one's complete rejection and disassociation with them, and as a means to expunge any demonic activity to which they were attached. Also, when by our words we come into agreement with something of an evil nature, by our words (spoken aloud) we also need to come out of agreement.

If you are a pastor of a church, which has allowed the martial arts or yoga to come in, I recommend that you repent before your entire congregation, and ask their forgiveness, as well as God's forgiveness. Then ask them to join with you in breaking the power of anything and everything that was given access through this open doorway into the lives of all who are in your congregation.

Command that all evil spirits leave and never return in Jesus' name! Obviously, anyone in your church, but especially anyone in any leadership position, who is involved in either of these activities should be willing to give them up or leave the church. It is spiritual adultery and not to be taken lightly.

May the Lord give you great knowledge, wisdom, discernment, and understanding in the days ahead, and may He use you to help others get ready for His Second Coming. May you continue to walk in His ways and "hear and obey" until the day of His imminent return. Jesus is coming back for a radiant, glorious bride without spot or wrinkle.

I would be remiss if I did not ask you this question. Do you know Jesus? Are you ready for His return? If you do not know Jesus in a personal way, but you would like to, then I urge you to repeat this prayer from your heart right now, to begin your walk with Him:

"Father God, I know I am not right with you and I would like your forgiveness. First and foremost, I confess that I am a sinner and I desire to know you through your son, Jesus, in a personal way. Come into my heart and change me so that when Jesus comes back soon, I'll be ready. Thank you...Amen!"

Notes

1. USA Today article by Henry G. Brinton titled "Body & Soul" 4 December 2006
2. Ibid.
3. Ibid.
4. USA Today article by Henry G. Brinton titled "Fitness & Faith" 4 December 2006
5. Ibid.
6. Ibid.
7. From website article by Joseph Agius, "A Christian Response: Christianity and Martial Arts: Are They Compatible? 8 December 2008 http://www.pastor.net.au/response/articles/144.htm

8. From website article by Biblical Discernment Ministries, "A Christian Response: Karate – Tool for Christian Evangelism or Zen Buddhism?" 8 December 2008 http://www.pastornet.net.au/response/articles/22.htm

9. Ibid.

10. From website article "Bruce Lee and Martial Arts: A Christian Perspective" 8 December 2008 <www.pastornet.net.au/response/articles/135.htm>

11. From website promoting Billy Blanks: Tae Bo Believer's Workout Strength Within – DVD, 30 December 2008 <http://www.christiancinema.com/catalog/product_info.php?products_id=2278>

12. Ibid.

13. Ibid.

Suggested Prayer to Renounce the Martial Arts

Father God, I come to you in the name of Jesus and because of His shed blood on my behalf. I repent for all my involvement in the martial arts. I bind and break the power of all evil spirits behind the martial arts, in any of its forms, and under any of its various names, and I renounce and reject them right now in Jesus' name. I break the power of every ungodly yoke that was formed in my life through this practice. I renounce believing in the "ki" or "ch'i," which I now know to be demonic strength and power.

I confess and I repent that I have sought to learn the martial arts because of a desire to protect myself or because of fear of sudden attack (or whatever other reason(s) – name them). Through this practice I have sought for revenge and to hurt people; I have also sought to gain prestige among men. I ask you to forgive me for all these sins and cleanse me with the blood of Jesus.

I repent for having established wrong relationships (soul ties) with fellow students and instructors, which were contrary to the Word of God, which says I am to have no fellowship with the works of darkness. I confess that I have idolized instructors, champions, founders, fellow practitioners, and myself, and I ask You to please forgive me of this idolatry.

I also renounce all trophies and rank I received in any martial art. I vow to destroy my belt, insignia, practice uniform, trophy, medal, certificate, achievement awards, membership card of any art or cultic organizations, book, poster, picture, films, swords or other weapons, and all other articles pertaining to the martial arts I have been involved in.

Father God, I ask you to forgive me. I renounce the pride, arrogance, intimidation, fear, rebellion, cruelty, violence, deception, manipulation, control, practice of divination, belief in false religions, movies based on martial arts, meditation through empty mindedness, any and all occult practices, which were part and parcel of the martial arts. I renounce the martial arts belief that it is an honorable thing, and that suicide is honorable. (If applicable, right now forgive anyone who may have been responsible for introducing you to the martial arts.)

I repent for any influence my involvement may have had on my spouse and/or my children. I break the power of this influence off of them right now in Jesus' name and the effects off my children generationally. I break every ungodly soul tie with anyone that was formed through any and all of my martial arts activities, including: (Name the names of people you have been involved with, and name each of the martial arts you have been involved in.)

I now command any and all evil spirits of pride, deception, divination and all occult spirits, rebellion, fear, violence, anger, hatred, cruelty, the Bushido warrior spirit, the dragon spirit, idolatry, and aggression to leave me now and remain gone in the name of Jesus Christ of Nazareth. I break the power of unbelief, as well as spiritual blindness and compromise that all of these things brought into my life. I now cancel any and all legal rights that evil spirits had to my life. I bind the power of all retaliation, revenge, and counter attack against myself, my family, my pets, or anything in my possession.

I ask you, Father God, to enforce my decision in the spirit realm and in the natural realm by the power of your Holy Spirit. Give me a hunger and thirst for your truth and your peace, which comes from meditating only on your Word. Please repair any damage that I did to my body and restore it back to normal. Remove any ill effects, deception, infirmities, and the veil of blindness that came in through this practice. Help me to fully understand your will and your ways, and walk in them from this day forward. I thank you, Father, in Jesus' name.

Suggested Prayer to Renounce Yoga & Transcendental Meditation

Father God, I come to you in the name of Jesus and because of His shed blood. I repent for my involvement in yoga, in any of its forms, and/or TM. I now bind and break the power of all evil spirits behind the practice of TM or yoga (in any of its forms and under any of its names) and I renounce and reject them right now in Jesus' name. I break the power of every ungodly yoke and soul tie that was formed in my life through this practice. I bind and break the power of the spirit of Kundalini. I vow to destroy any and all objects associated with this practice.

I renounce believing in the "prana" which I now know to be demonic empowerment. I renounce believing in this kind of meditation as being able to relieve me of stress, bring peace and health benefits into my life, and achieve any kind of enlightenment, self-awareness, or oneness with the universe. I renounce belief in meridians, chakras, karma, nirvana, reincarnation, and mantras.

Forgive me, Father God, for believing that there was no danger in this practice and for blanking out my mind, which allowed the enemy of my soul access into my life. I renounce all the positions and postures that I participated in and everything they were symbolic of, and all mantras, which I spoke.

I now recognize that any and all spiritual powers associated with any yoga or TM practice come from the demonic realm. I now break the demonic power off my life and I break all demonic yokes of bondage. I sever completely any and all connection in the spirit realm to all Hindu (or New Age) beliefs and all Hindu gods, which I now know is based on the occult and false religious practices. I blind the third eye of the medium and all psychic sight.

I now command any and all evil spirits associated with TM or yoga, including the Kundalini (serpent force), all those posing as false peace and serenity, all spirit guides that came through meditation, divination, deception, and infirmities that came in through this doorway to leave me now and never return in the name of Jesus Christ of Nazareth! I now cancel any and all legal rights that evil spirits had to my life.

I bind and break the power of this influence that yoga or TM may have brought to my spouse, and/or my children, and I break all generational effects off my children now. I bind the power of all retaliation, revenge, and counter attack against myself, my family, my pets, or anything in my possession.

I ask you, Father God, to enforce my decision in the spirit realm, and in the natural realm, by the power of your Holy Spirit. Give me a hunger and thirst for your truth and your peace, which comes from meditating only on your Word. Please repair any damage that may have been done to my nervous system, and remove all ill effects, deception, infirmities, and the veil of blindness that came in through this practice. Help me to fully understand your will and your ways, and walk in them from this day forward. I thank you, Father, in Jesus' name!

To Contact the Author

Dr. Vito Rallo
Free Indeed Ministries of Tampa Bay
P. O. Box 651
Riverview, FL 33568-0651

Email: prallo@msn.com

Websites:
www.secretsbehindmartialarts.com
www.freeindeedministries.org

OTHER RESOURCES BY VITO AND PATRICIA RALLO

Available from:
www.freeindeedministries.org

Heaven Bound: Are You Sure?
by Vito & Pat Rallo

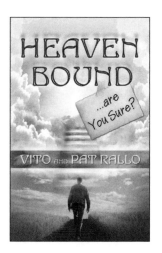

Is it the spirit or soul of man that must be "born again?" Can a person know for sure they are heaven bound? Will praying a "sinner's prayer," water baptism, doing good works, or faithful church attendance save you? What does God require? How can a good God send anyone to hell? Have you asked these or similar questions? In answering these questions, and more, Vito and Pat thoroughly examine what the Bible says versus what many have implied or taught. In this book, you will discover 15 "revelation secrets" straight from the throne room of God.

Breaking Generational Curses & Pulling Down Strongholds

by Vito Rallo

(available in book & audio book)

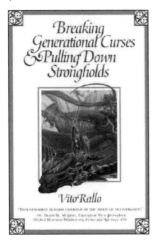

Find out how to avoid the dangerous snares, traps, and pitfalls that people can fall into if they are unaware of the devil's tactics. This book will walk you through the necessary steps to pull down any sin patterns (strongholds) you may have in your own life or generational iniquities you may have inherited as so much unwanted "spiritual baggage." You will come out in a place of victory and freedom in Christ!

This is Not a Dress Rehearsal!

by Patricia Rallo

(available in book and audio book)

The urgency of the hour has never been more real. Whether you are in church, out of church, have never been to church, or have given up on church, this book will answer burning questions you may have had for a long time. Some difficult topics are addressed within its pages. You will find it full of wisdom and practical ways of how to be an overcomer. We are living in the dramatic end times! Where do you fit in the last days' drama?

Walking in Freedom

by Vito & Pat Rallo

(audio from a Freedom Seminar) 5-CD set

This is a powerful conference that every believer will want to hear. Vito and Pat Rallo are a dynamic "tag-team" as they minister in the areas of inner healing and deliverance. Walk out your victory from past rejections and abuse as you participate in the altar calls and renunciation prayers. Vito & Pat both share powerful testimonies. The occult is exposed during this teaching and you will learn how to rid your home of any demonic symbols. Learn the truth about the spirit behind freemasonry, as well as Roman Catholicism.

Recommended
by Sovereign World

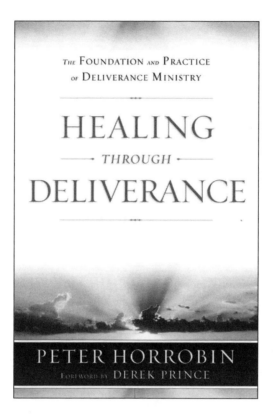

Healing through Deliverance
The foundation & Practice of Deliverance Ministry
(hardback)
Peter Horrobin

UK List: £24.99 (Published by Sovereign World)
US List: $29.99 (North America edition published by Chosen)
Pages: 586pp

In this groundbreaking volume, Peter draws on his experience to set out a thorough scriptural foundation for the healing and deliverance ministry—an integral part of fulfilling the Great Commission and a vital key to discipleship. He lays out the biblical basis for healing through deliverance; provides safe guidelines and practical tools for building a healing and deliverance ministry; helps people identify possible demonic entry points; and teaches how we can become affected by demonic power and how we can be delivered and healed.

Discover more titles from Sovereign World
The Truth & Freedom Series

Rescue from Rejection: Finding Security in God's Loving Acceptance
Denise Cross
£7.99 / $13.99 / 160pp

The Dangers of Alternative Ways to Healing: How to Avoid New Age Deceptions
David Cross & John Berry
£8.99 / $14.99 / 176pp

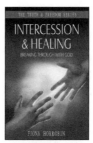

Intercession & Healing: Breaking Through with God
Fiona Horrobin
£7.99 / $14.99/ 176pp

Hope & Healing for the Abused
Paul & Liz Griffin
£6.99 / $10.99 / 128pp

Trapped by Control: How To Find Freedom
David Cross
£6.99 / $10.99 / 112pp

Anger: How Do You Handle It?
Paul & Liz Griffin
£6.99 / $10.99 / 112pp

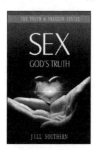

Sex: God's Truth
Jill Southern
£6.99 / $10.99 / 128pp

Soul Ties: The Unseen Bond in Relationships
David Cross
£6.99 / $10.99 / 128pp

God's Covering: A Place of Healing
David Cross
£7.99 / $14.99 / 192pp

For more information about these titles visit:
www.sovereignworld.com